History 2
Student Guide

Part 2

About K12 Inc.

K12 Inc., a technology-based education company, is the nation's leading provider of proprietary curriculum and online education programs to students in grades K–12. K^{12} provides its curriculum and academic services to online schools, traditional classrooms, blended school programs, and directly to families. K12 Inc. also operates the K^{12} International Academy, an accredited, diploma-granting online private school serving students worldwide. K^{12}'s mission is to provide any child the curriculum and tools to maximize success in life, regardless of geographic, financial, or demographic circumstances. K12 Inc. is accredited by CITA. More information can be found at www.K12.com.

Table of Contents

Student Guide
Lesson 1: Threat from the North: Viking Warriors on the Move

Return to Europe to visit the northern lands of the Vikings, whose swift ships carried them far out into the world. Learn how these fierce warriors became explorers and traders. Then meet some Viking heroes, and learn more about their beliefs and traditions.

After Charlemagne's death, [NGT]his empire was beset by infighting and a new threat from the north. Bands of Norse warriors, called Vikings, began raiding the coastal and inland river villages of Europe.

Lesson Objectives
- Demonstrate mastery of important knowledge and skills taught in previous lessons.
- Explain that Viking raiders traveled in long, swift ships that often had carved dragon heads.
- Identify Vikings as fierce raiders and warriors.
- Explain that Vikings came from the north.

PREPARE

Approximate lesson time is 60 minutes.

Materials
For the Student

    🖳 map of Viking Lands, 800-1100 A.D.

Optional

    🖳 Viking Raiders activity sheet

    🖳 Viking Ship activity sheet

    pencils, no. 2

    paper, 8 1/2" x 11"

    pencils, colored, 16 or more

    crayons, 16 or more

    markers, colored, 8 or more

    🖳 map of Viking Lands, 800-1100 A.D

Keywords and Pronunciation
berserker (bur-ZUR-kur)

berserkers (bur-ZUR-kurz)

Vikings : Scandinavian people who raided the coasts of northern and western Europe from the eighth through the tenth century.

LEARN
Activity 1: Europe in the Middle Ages *(Online)*

Activity 2: The Days of the Vikings *(Online)*

Activity 3: Show You Know *(Online)*

Activity 4: History Record Book *(Online)*

Activity 5. Optional: My Viking Ship *(Online)*

Activity 6: Viking Raiders *(Online)*

ASSESS

Lesson Assessment: Threat from the North: Viking Warriors on the Move (*Online*)

You will complete an offline assessment covering the main objectives of this lesson. Your learning coach will score this assessment.

LEARN
Activity 7. Optional: More About the Vikings *(Online)*

Viking Lands, 800-1100 A.D.

N

ICELAND

FAEROE ISLANDS

ATLANTIC
OCEAN

SCANDINAVIA

FINLAND

RUSSIA

IRELAND

BRITAIN

English Channel

Rhine River

Seine River

Normandy

KINGDOM OF
THE FRANKS

Constantinople

BYZANTINE
EMPIRE

0 miles   300 miles

Viking Raiders Activity Sheet

Use the word bank to complete each caption. Color the Viking pictures.

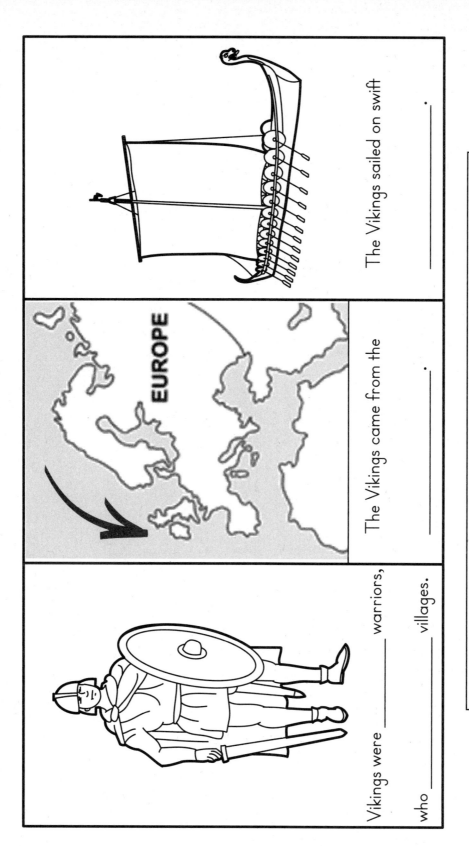

The Vikings sailed on swift _____.

The Vikings came from the _____.

Vikings were _____ warriors, who _____ villages.

Word Bank: ships   rafts   north   south   fierce   calm   helped   raided

Answers: Panel 1: fierce, raided   Panel 2: north   Panel 3: ships

Name _____   Date _____

Viking Ship Coloring Sheet

Color this classic Viking ship. When you are finished, write a caption for your picture. "Viking ships were......"

Viking ships were _____.

Viking Raiders Activity Sheet

Use the word bank to complete each caption. Color the Viking pictures.

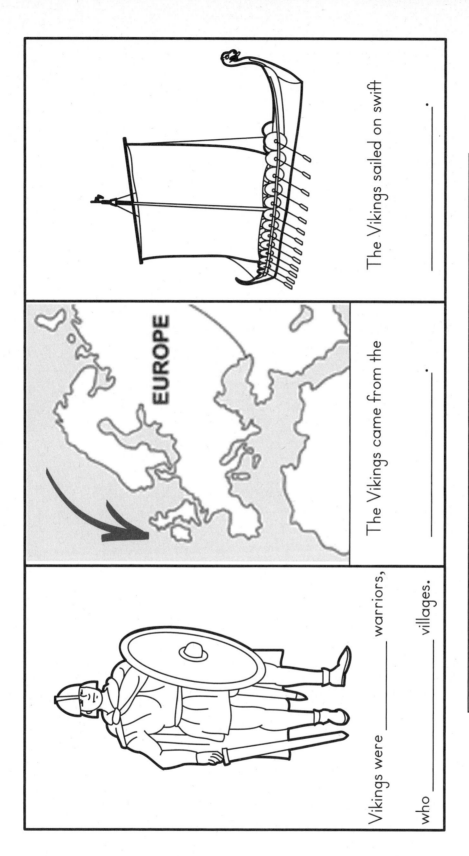

The Vikings sailed on swift _____.

The Vikings came from the _____.

Vikings were _____ warriors, who _____ villages.

Word Bank: ships   rafts   north   south   fierce   calm   helped   raided

Answers: Panel 1: fierce, raided   Panel 2: north   Panel 3: ships

Name _____   Date _____

Viking Ship Coloring Sheet

Color this classic Viking ship. When you are finished, write a caption for your picture. "Viking ships were......"

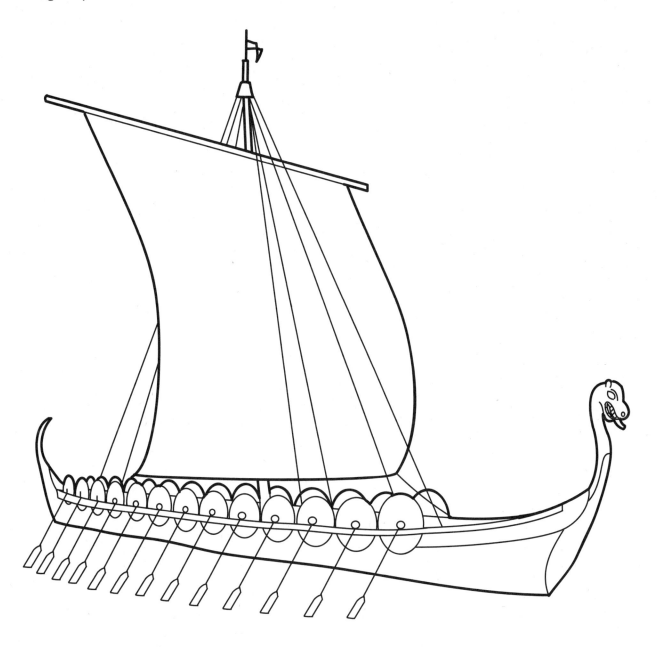

Viking ships were _____.

Lesson Assessment

Threat from the North: Viking Warriors on the Move

1. What is the name of the fierce warriors we learned about today?

2. Did the Vikings come from the north or the south?

3. What might you expect to see carved on the front of a Viking ship?

4. What did the Vikings do to villages they raided?

Student Guide
Lesson 2: Viking Shipbuilders and Explorers

The Vikings lived in Scandinavia. Their swift, light longships carried raiders, traders, and explorers far and wide, even to North America.

Lesson Objectives

- Demonstrate mastery of important knowledge and skills taught in previous lessons.
- Locate Scandinavia on a map.
- Recognize a Viking ship.
- Identify Erik the Red and Leif Eriksson as Viking explorers.

PREPARE

Approximate lesson time is 60 minutes.

Materials

For the Student

 map of Viking Lands, 800-1100 A.D.

Optional

 Leif Eriksson and Erik the Red Activity Sheet

 Viking Ship activity sheet

globe, inflatable

pencils, no. 2

paper, 8 1/2" x 11"

pencils, colored, 16 or more

crayons, 16 or more

scissors, round-end safety

Growing Up in Viking Times by Dominic Tweddle

Keywords and Pronunciation

Leif Eriksson (leef EHR-ik-suhn)

Scandinavia : A region of northern Europe consisting of Norway, Sweden, and Denmark. It is sometimes said to include Finland, Iceland, and the Faeroe Islands.

LEARN
Activity 1: Who Were the Vikings? *(Online)*

Activity 2: Sailing with the Vikings *(Online)*

Activity 3: Show You Know *(Online)*

Activity 4: History Record Book *(Online)*

Activity 5. Optional: Leif Eriksson's Ship *(Online)*

Activity 6. Optional: Just Where Is Scandinavia? *(Online)*

ASSESS

Lesson Assessment: Viking Shipbuilders and Explorers (*Online*)

You will complete an offline assessment covering the main objectives of this lesson. Your learning coach will score this assessment.

LEARN

Activity 7. Optional: Learn More About Vikings *(Online)*

Viking Lands, 800-1100 A.D.

N

ICELAND

FAEROE ISLANDS

ATLANTIC
OCEAN

SCANDINAVIA

FINLAND

RUSSIA

IRELAND

BRITAIN

English Channel

Rhine River

Seine River

Normandy

KINGDOM OF
THE FRANKS

Constantinople

BYZANTINE
EMPIRE

0 miles   300 miles

Viking Raiders Activity Sheet

Use the word bank to complete each caption. Color the Viking pictures.

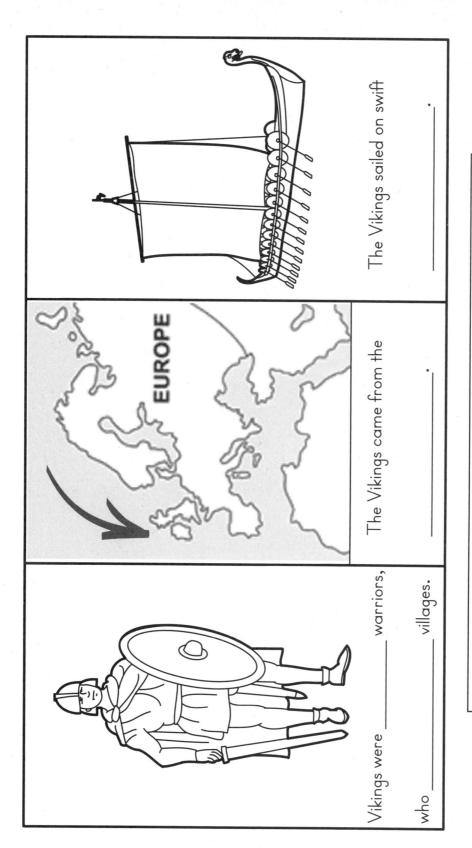

The Vikings sailed on swift _____ .

The Vikings came from the _____ .

Vikings were _____ warriors, who _____ villages.

Word Bank: ships   rafts   north   south   fierce   calm   helped   raided

Answers: Panel 1: fierce, raided   Panel 2: north   Panel 3: ships

Name _____   Date _____

Viking Ship Activity Sheet

Name the parts of this Viking ship using words from the word bank. Color the ship, and add some special details of your own.

Word Bank:	keel,	sail,	prow,	oars

Lesson Assessment

Viking Shipbuilders and Explorers

1. Point to Scandinavia on the map.

2. Which of these ships is a Viking ship?

3. Who were Erik the Red and Leif Eriksson?

Viking Lands, 800-1100 A.D.

N

ICELAND

FAEROE ISLANDS

ATLANTIC
OCEAN

SCANDINAVIA

FINLAND

RUSSIA

IRELAND

BRITAIN

English Channel

Rhine River

Seine River

Normandy

KINGDOM OF
THE FRANKS

Constantinople

BYZANTINE
EMPIRE

0 miles   300 miles

Student Guide
Lesson 3: Viking Life

Follow a young Norse girl as she goes about her morning chores, awaits her father's return from voyages abroad and learns about runes.

Lesson Objectives

- Demonstrate mastery of important knowledge and skills taught in previous lessons.
- Recognize Viking runes from a picture.
- Describe the Vikings as traders.
- Identify the Vikings as people who lived near fjords.
- Explain that the letters of the Viking alphabet are called runes.

PREPARE

Approximate lesson time is 60 minutes.

Materials

For the Student

    🖳 map of Viking Lands, 800-1100 A.D.

    🖳 Runes: The Viking Alphabet sheet

Optional

    🖳 Fjords and Beyond activity sheet

    globe, inflatable

    pencils, no. 2

    paper, 8 1/2" x 11"

    pencils, colored, 16 or more

    Play-Doh

    crayons, 16 or more

    Who Were the Vikings? by Jane Chisholm et al

Keywords and Pronunciation

Astrid (AHS-trid)

Bjorn (byourn)

fjord (fee-AWRD) : Steep-sided inlet of the sea.

rune : Any of the characters in several alphabets used by ancient Germanic peoples.

runes (roons)

LEARN
Activity 1: Reviewing Facts About Vikings *(Online)*

Activity 2: Learn About Viking Life *(Online)*

Activity 3: Show You Know *(Online)*

Activity 4: History Record Book *(Online)*

Activity 5. Optional: Writing with Runes *(Online)*

Activity 6. Optional: Fjords and Beyond *(Online)*

ASSESS

Lesson Assessment: Viking Life (*Online*)
You will complete an offline assessment covering the main objectives of this lesson. Your learning coach will score this assessment.

LEARN
Activity 7. Optional: Read More About Vikings *(Online)*

Runes: The Viking Alphabet

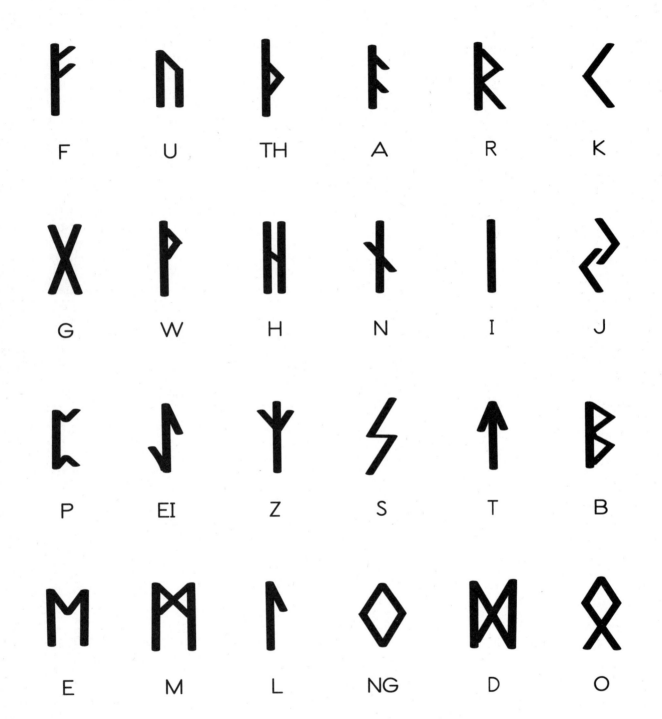

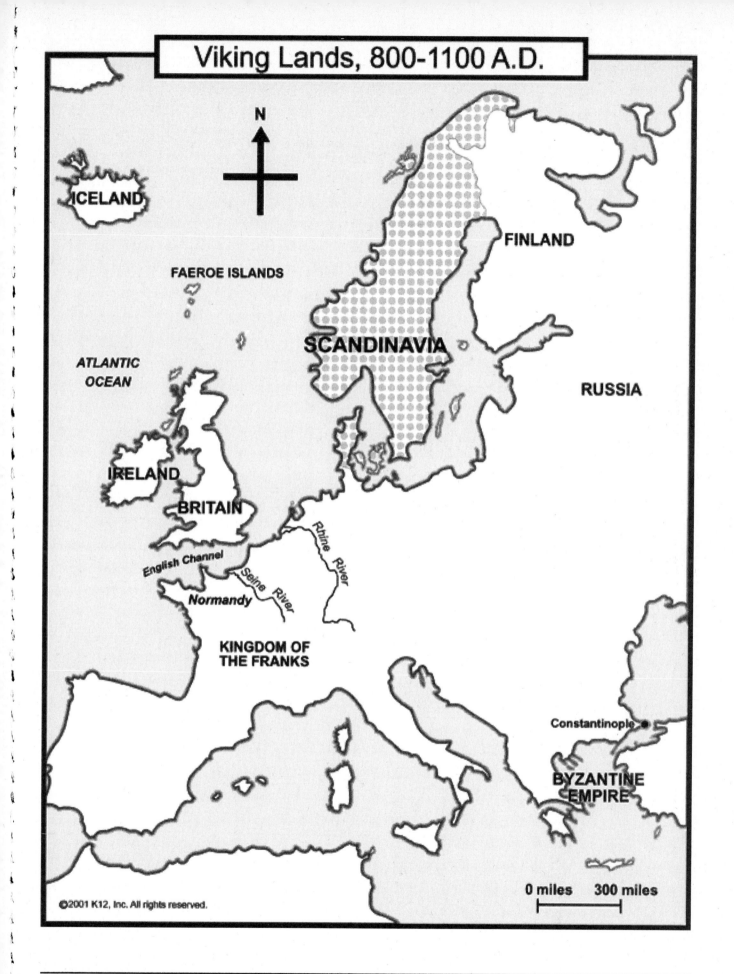

Viking Lands, 800-1100 A.D.

N

ICELAND

FAEROE ISLANDS

ATLANTIC
OCEAN

SCANDINAVIA

FINLAND

RUSSIA

IRELAND

BRITAIN

English Channel

Seine River

Rhine River

Normandy

KINGDOM OF
THE FRANKS

Constantinople

BYZANTINE
EMPIRE

0 miles   300 miles

Name _____   **Date** _____

Fjords and Beyond

Think back to what you learned about how the Vikings sailed out of the fjords into the world beyond. They began as raiders but became famous as traders. Where did they go, and what did they trade? Color the mountains, the fjord, and the ship sailing out of it. Then look at the list of goods and places below. Cross off the ones that were not a part of Viking trade.

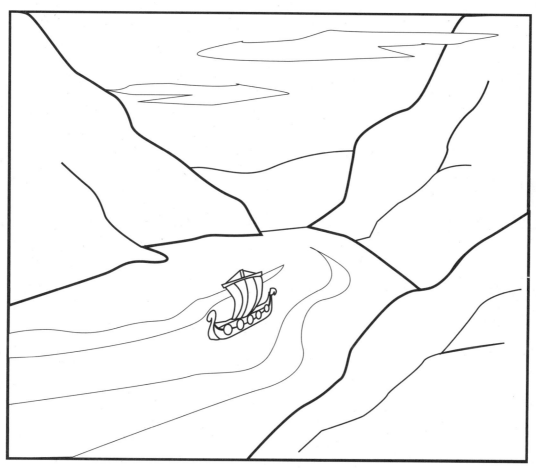

Places the Vikings Traded	
Russia	Antarctica
Brazil	Byzantine Empire
Baghdad	Mexico
Constantinople	

Goods the Vikings Traded	
furs	white bears
honey	alligators
crayons	glass
silver	

Lesson Assessment

Viking Life

1. When the Vikings raided a village, what did they do with many of the things they stole?

2. Where did the Vikings build their villages?

3. What were Viking letters called?

4. What does this picture show?

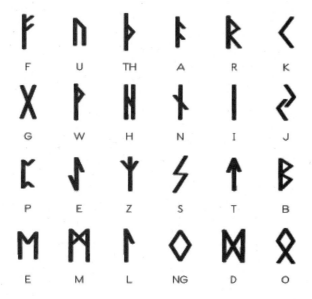

Runes: The Viking Alphabet

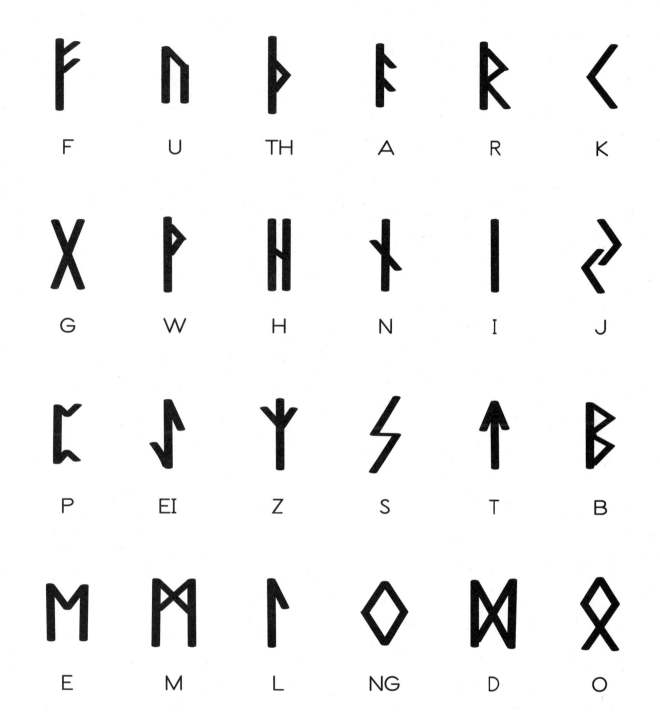

Student Guide
Lesson 4: Viking Gods and Goddesses

The Vikings believed in many gods and goddesses, from a powerful thunder god to a god of war. Today, our names for certain days of the week are reminders of the Norse gods.

Lesson Objectives

- Demonstrate mastery of important knowledge and skills taught in previous lessons.
- Identify Asgard as the land of the Viking gods and goddesses.
- Name at least two days of the week that are named for Viking gods or goddesses and the god or goddess each is named for.
- Explain that the Vikings believed in many gods and goddesses.
- Name at least two of the Viking gods or goddesses.

PREPARE

Approximate lesson time is 60 minutes.

Materials

For the Student
Optional

    📇 A Viking's Week activity sheet
    📇 Viking Gods and Goddesses activity sheet
    globe, inflatable
    pencils, no. 2
    paper, 8 1/2" x 11"
    pencils, colored, 16 or more
    crayons, 16 or more
    brush, watercolor
    paints, watercolor, 8 colors or more
    Play-Doh - red or yellow
    scissors, round-end safety
    yarn - about 24 inches

Keywords and Pronunciation

Asgard (AS-gahrd)
Freya (FRAY-uh)
Loki (LOH-kee)
Odin (OH-dn)
Tyr (tihr)

LEARN
Activity 1: Scandinavia *(Online)*

Activity 2: Viking Gods and Goddesses *(Online)*

Activity 3: How Thor Got His Hammer *(Online)*

Activity 4: Show You Know *(Online)*

Activity 5: History Record Book *(Online)*

Activity 6. Optional: A Viking's Week *(Online)*

Activity 7. Optional: The Land of Asgard *(Online)*

ASSESS

Lesson Assessment: Viking Gods and Goddesses (*Online*)

You will complete an offline assessment covering the main objectives of this lesson. Your learning coach will score this assessment.

LEARN
Activity 8. Optional: Thor's Hammer *(Online)*

Viking Gods and Goddesses

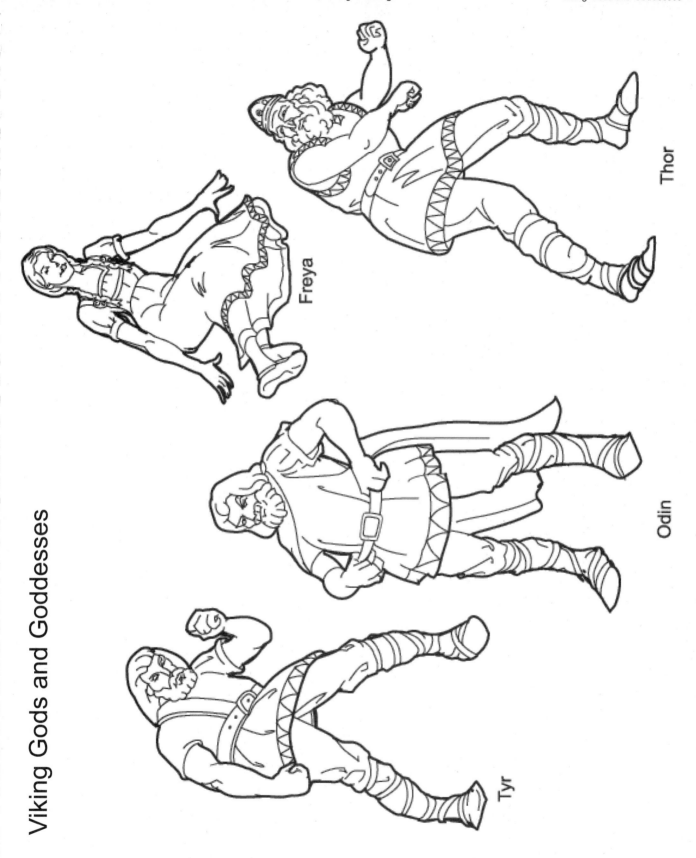

Thor

Freya

Odin

Tyr

A Viking's Week

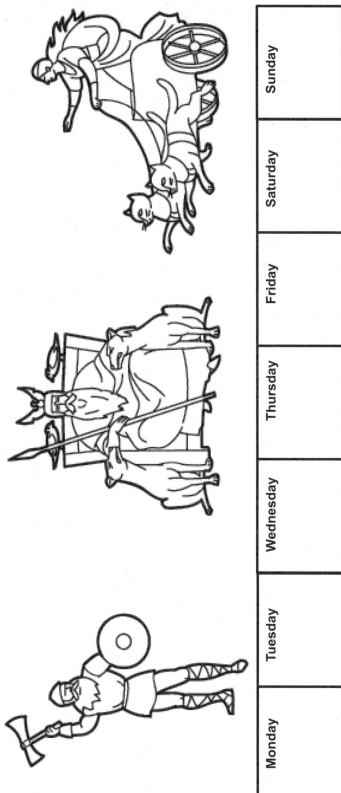

Monday	Tuesday	Wednesday	Thursday	Friday	Saturday	Sunday

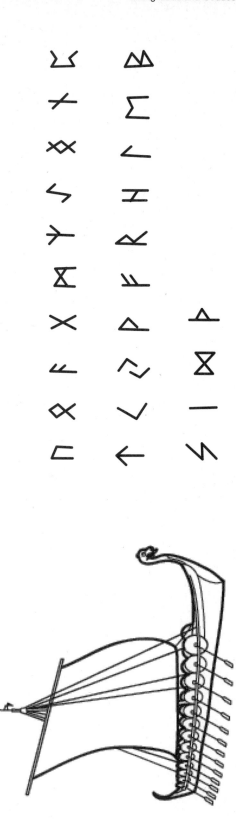

Name _____   Date _____

Lesson Assessment

Viking Gods and Goddesses

1. Did the Vikings believe in one God, or in many gods and goddesses?

2. Name as many Viking gods and goddesses as you can.

3. Name as many days of the week named for Viking gods and goddesses as you can, and the god or goddess each is named for.

4. What was the land of the Viking gods and goddesses called?

Student Guide
Lesson 5: Buried in Style

Viking warriors wanted to go to the mythical realm of Valhalla when they died. Some Vikings who died were laid in ships with clothing, jewelry, and animals to take with them to Valhalla. These great ships were often buried.

Lesson Objectives
- Demonstrate mastery of important knowledge and skills taught in previous lessons.
- Identify Valhalla as Odin's palace.
- Explain that Viking warriors wanted to go to Valhalla when they died.
- Describe Viking burial ships as containing things the dead would need in the afterlife.

PREPARE

Approximate lesson time is 60 minutes.

Materials
For the Student
Optional
- 💻 Valhalla: Odin's Palace activity sheet
- 💻 Viking Burial Ship activity sheet
- 💻 Viking Warrior activity sheet
  - globe, inflatable
  - pencils, no. 2
  - paper, 8 1/2" x 11"
  - pencils, colored, 16 or more
  - glue sticks
  - scissors, round-end safety
  - crayons, 16 or more
  - paper, colored construction, 12"x12" - brown
  - Elmer's Glue-All
  - markers, colored, 8 or more
  - shoeboxes

Keywords and Pronunciation
Valhalla (val-HA-luh)
Valkyries (val-KIHR-ees)

LEARN
Activity 1: Viking Gods and Goddesses *(Online)*

Activity 2: Afterlife in Asgard *(Online)*

Activity 3: Show You Know *(Online)*

Activity 4: History Record Book *(Online)*

Activity 5. Optional: Fill the Viking Burial Ship *(Online)*

Activity 6. Optional: Valhalla: Odin's Palace *(Online)*

ASSESS
Lesson Assessment: Buried in Style (*Online*)
You will complete an offline assessment covering the main objectives of this lesson. Your learning coach will score this assessment.

LEARN
Activity 7. Optional: Make a Viking Ship *(Online)*

A Viking Burial Ship

A Viking burial ship contained things the dead would need in the afterlife. Color each item. Cut each item out and add it to the ship above.

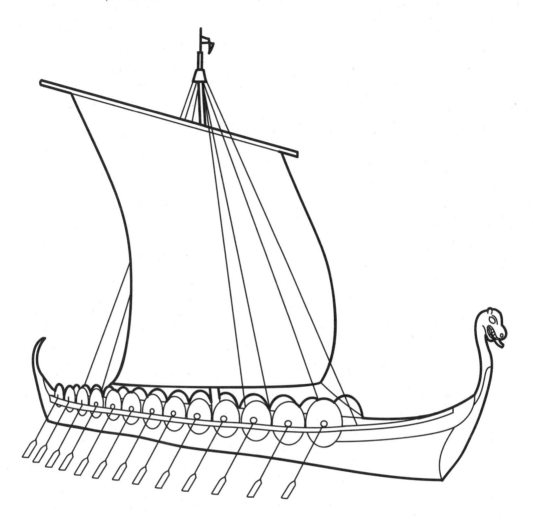

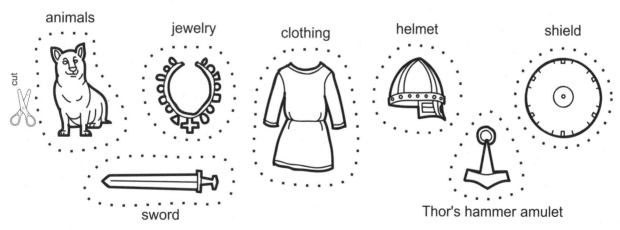

animals

jewelry

clothing

helmet

shield

cut

sword

Thor's hammer amulet

Viking Warrior Cut-Out Sheet

Lesson Assessment

Buried in Style

1. Where did Viking warriors want to go when they died?

2. What was the name of Odin's palace in Asgard?

3. What did the Vikings put in the burial ships along with their dead?

Student Guide
Lesson 6: The Normans Invade England

When a group of Vikings settled in northwestern France, they became known as "Normans," and the land they settled, "Normandy." Years after their settlement, a Norman named William came to power, attacked England, and won the English crown for himself.

Lesson Objectives

- Demonstrate mastery of important knowledge and skills taught in previous lessons.
- Name William the Conqueror as the leader who led the Normans to conquer England.
- Locate Normandy on a map.
- Explain that Vikings who settled in northern France were called Normans.

PREPARE

Approximate lesson time is 60 minutes.

Materials

> For the Student
> Optional
>> 🖥 map of Viking Lands, 800-1100 A.D.
>> globe, inflatable
>> pencils, no. 2
>> paper, 8 1/2" x 11"
>> pencils, colored, 16 or more
>> crayons, 16 or more
>> Elmer's Glue-All
>> glitter - gold
>> glitter - silver
>> index cards, 4" x 6"
>> Artists' Workshop: Stories by Penny King and Claire Roundhill

Keywords and Pronunciation

Seine (sen)

LEARN
Activity 1: Viking Afterlife *(Online)*

Activity 2: The Land of Normandy (Online)

Activity 3: Show You Know (Online)

Activity 4: History Record Book (Online)

Activity 5. Optional: William's Map (Online)

Activity 6. Optional: Normandy Memory Game (Online)

ASSESS

Lesson Assessment: The Normans Invade England (Online)

You will complete an offline assessment covering the main objectives of this lesson. Your learning coach will score this assessment.

LEARN

Activity 7. Optional: Bayeux Tapestry (Online)

Viking Lands, 800-1100 A.D.

N

ICELAND

FAEROE ISLANDS

ATLANTIC OCEAN

IRELAND

BRITAIN

English Channel

Seine River

Normandy

Rhine River

KINGDOM OF THE FRANKS

SCANDINAVIA

FINLAND

RUSSIA

Constantinople

BYZANTINE EMPIRE

0 miles   300 miles

Viking Lands, 800-1100 A.D.

N

ICELAND

FAEROE ISLANDS

FINLAND

SCANDINAVIA

ATLANTIC
OCEAN

RUSSIA

IRELAND

BRITAIN

English Channel

Rhine River

Seine River

Normandy

KINGDOM OF
THE FRANKS

Constantinople

BYZANTINE
EMPIRE

0 miles   300 miles

Lesson Assessment

The Normans Invade England

1. Point to Normandy on the map.

2. When the Vikings settled in northern France, what were they called?

3. Who was the leader who led the Normans to conquer England?

Viking Lands, 800-1100 A.D.

N

ICELAND

FAEROE ISLANDS

ATLANTIC
OCEAN

SCANDINAVIA

FINLAND

RUSSIA

IRELAND

BRITAIN

English Channel

Rhine River

Seine River

Normandy

KINGDOM OF
THE FRANKS

Constantinople

BYZANTINE
EMPIRE

0 miles   300 miles

Student Guide
Lesson 7: Sigurd: A Viking Hero

Meet Sigurd, a Norse hero, and follow him on his quest to slay a terrible dragon.

Lesson Objectives
- Demonstrate mastery of important knowledge and skills taught in previous lessons.
- Demonstrate mastery of important knowledge and skills in this unit.
- Locate Scandinavia on a map.
- Identify Sigurd as a Viking hero.

PREPARE

Approximate lesson time is 60 minutes.

Materials
> For the Student
> Optional
> > 🖳 Viking Gods and Heros
> > 🖳 Dragon Slayer activity sheet
> > glue sticks
> > paper, colored construction, 12"x12"
> > pencils, colored, 16 or more
> > scissors, round-end safety

Keywords and Pronunciation
Fafnir (FAHV-nuhr)
Sigurd (SIH-gourd)

LEARN
Activity 1: Viking Review *(Online)*

Activity 2: Unit Review: A World in Turmoil *(Online)*

ASSESS

Unit Assessment: A World in Turmoil (*Offline*)
You will complete an offline assessment covering the main objectives of this lesson. Your learning coach will score this assessment.

LEARN
Activity 3. Optional: Sigurd, the Hero (Online)

Activity 4. Optional: Sigurd the Dragon Slayer (Online)

SIGURD

Name _____   Date _____

The Viking Challenge

Read each sentence and its answer choices. Fill in the bubble in front the word or words that best answer the question.

1. Which of the following are all Viking gods?
    - ○ Loki, Thor, Odin
    - ○ Eric, Tyr, Athena
    - ○ Zeus, Leif, Freya

2. How would you describe Vikings?
    - ○ gentle farmers and herders
    - ○ fierce raiders and warriors
    - ○ wise teachers and doctors

3. From which direction did the Vikings come?
    - ○ north
    - ○ south
    - ○ west

4. Who were Eric the Red and Leif Eriksson?
    - ○ Norman warriors
    - ○ Viking explorers
    - ○ Saxon kings

5. Where did Viking warriors hope to go when they died?
    - ○ to a watery grave
    - ○ to Odin's palace named Valhalla
    - ○ to an island in the North Sea

6. Who was the Norman who led his soldiers in battle against England and became its king?
   - ○ Sigurd the Dragon Slayer
   - ○ Thor the Hammer
   - ○ William the Conqueror

7. What was the name of the land of the Viking gods and goddesses?
   - ○ Asgard
   - ○ Greenland
   - ○ Scandinavia

8. What did Viking raiders travel in?
   - ○ short, slow ships with carved bird heads
   - ○ short, swift ships with carved horse heads
   - ○ long, swift ships with carved dragon heads

9. What does this picture show?

   - ○ Greek symbols
   - ○ Egyptian hieroglyphs
   - ○ Viking runes

10. Point to Scandinavia on the map.

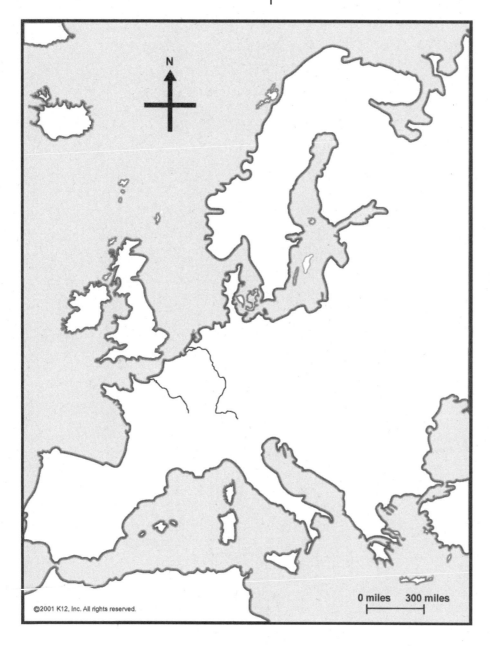

0 miles   300 miles

©2001 K12, Inc. All rights reserved.

Student Guide
Lesson 1: What Was Feudalism?

Learn about life in medieval castles and understand how the feudal world worked. Explore medieval times with some serfs, knights, nobles, and kings. Meet St. George; see a cathedral; enjoy a fair; and learn how one woman became queen of both England and France.

In medieval western Europe, feudalism became a way of life and provided some protection and stability. In the feudal system, people exchanged land, loyalty and service in return for protection.

Lesson Objectives

- Demonstrate mastery of important knowledge and skills taught in previous lessons.
- Describe feudalism.
- Identify feudalism as a system in which people exchanged land, loyalty, and service in return for protection.
- Identify a serf as a peasant who worked the land.
- List the order of rule in feudalism: king, noble, knight, serf.

PREPARE

Approximate lesson time is 60 minutes.

Materials

For the Student

Optional

- 🖥 Medieval Movie activity sheet
- 🖥 The Feudal Pyramid activity sheet
- 🖥 The People of Feudalism activity sheet

  pencils, no. 2

  paper, 8 1/2" x 11"

  pencils, colored, 16 or more

  crayons, 16 or more

  paper, colored construction, 12"x12"

  Elmer's Glue-All

  scissors, round-end safety

  markers, colored, 8 or more

  toys - chess game

  The Age of Feudalism by Timothy Levi Biel

Keywords and Pronunciation

feudalism (FYOO-dl-ih-zuhm) : A political or economic system in which people exchanged land, loyalty, and service in return for protection.

loyalty : Being true to a person or thing as promised.

serf : A member of the lowest feudal class.

LEARN
Activity 1: Review the Middle Ages *(Online)*

Activity 2: Charlemagne and the Middle Ages *(Online)*

Activity 3: Understanding Feudalism *(Online)*

Activity 4: Show You Know *(Online)*

Activity 5: History Record Book *(Online)*

Activity 6. Optional: The Feudal Pyramid *(Online)*

Activity 7. Optional: Medieval Movie *(Online)*

ASSESS

Lesson Assessment: What Was Feudalism? (*Online*)

You will complete an offline assessment covering the main objectives of this lesson. Your learning coach will score this assessment.

LEARN
Activity 8. Optional: Read More About Feudalism *(Online)*

Name

Date

Medieval Movie

Think of a title for your movie about feudalism. Write its name across the top or bottom of the page. On the back of this sheet, divide your paper into four equal parts. Add four more scenes to your movie. Show the main characters and some of the action you would like to see.

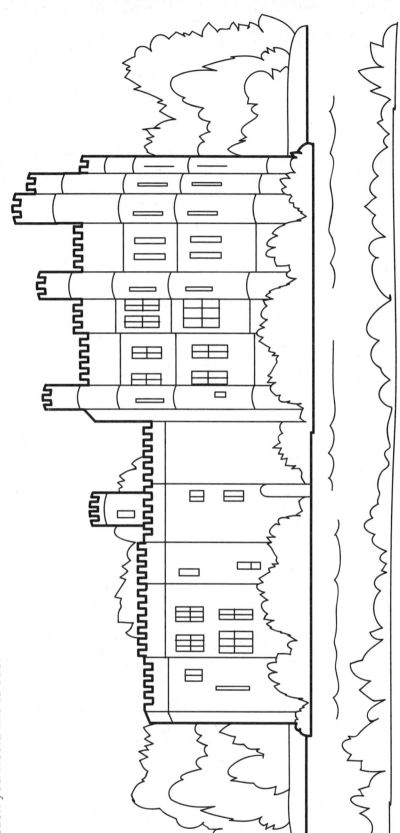

The People of Feudalism

Color the people of medieval times. Cut out the boxes holding them. Cut out the words naming their roles. Glue each of these titles to the figure(s) it names.

King	Nobles
Knights	Serfs

The Feudal Pyramid

Glue each box from
"The People of Feudalism" inside the
pyramid in the correct order.
Remember to put the most powerful
person at the top. Cut out the pyramid
and glue it to a piece of construction
paper. Decorate the border, and
write the word "Feudalism"
at the bottom.

The People of Feudalism

Color the people of medieval times. Cut out the boxes holding them. Cut out the words naming their roles. Glue each of these titles to the figure(s) it names.

King	Nobles
Knights	Serfs

Lesson Assessment

What Was Feudalism?

1. What is the name for the trade of land, loyalty, and service in return for protection?

2. Let's put these people in order from the person with the most power to the person with the least power: knight, serf, king, noble.

3. Who were the serfs?

4. Describe feudalism.

Student Guide
Lesson 2: Building a Castle

Castles were medieval fortress-homes. The first wooden castles quickly gave way to fortified stone castles.

Lesson Objectives
- Demonstrate mastery of important knowledge and skills taught in previous lessons.
- Explain that the first castles were made of wood.
- Identify the moat and drawbridge on a castle.
- Explain that stone castles were hard to attack.

PREPARE

Approximate lesson time is 60 minutes.

Materials

For the Student

Optional

    🖳 Catapult Directions activity sheet

    pencils, no. 2

    paper, 8 1/2" x 11"

    pencils, colored, 16 or more

    cardboard, sheets

    crayons, 16 or more

    paper, colored construction, 12"x12"

    toilet paper tubes

    brush, watercolor

    Elmer's Glue-All

    paints, watercolor, 8 colors or more

    scissors, round-end safety

    shoeboxes

    string

    beans, dried

    popsicle sticks

    rubber bands

    tape, masking

    A Three-Dimensional Medieval Castle by Willabel Tong

    Action Packs: Castle by Deni Brown

    Castle by DK Eyewitness Series

Keywords and Pronunciation

drawbridge : A bridge that can be raised to prevent access or to permit a boat or ship to pass beneath it.

medieval (meh-DEE-vuhl) : Having to do with the Middle Ages.

moat : A deep wide ditch, usually filled with water, which surrounds a building.

siege (seej)

LEARN
Activity 1: Reviewing Feudalism *(Online)*

Activity 2: The History of Castles *(Online)*

Activity 3: Castles Today *(Online)*

Activity 4: Show You Know *(Online)*

Activity 5: History Record Book *(Online)*

Activity 6. Optional: Build Your Own Castle *(Online)*

Activity 7. Optional: Catapult *(Online)*

ASSESS
Lesson Assessment: Building a Castle (*Online*)

You will complete an offline assessment covering the main objectives of this lesson. Your learning coach will score this assessment.

LEARN
Activity 8. Optional: Read More About Castles *(Online)*

Catapult Directions

Armies used catapults to attack castles during sieges. Make one of your own to learn how catapults worked. Gather the materials, follow the directions, and then use a dried bean to try out your medieval machine.

Materials:
2 toilet paper tubes
1 sheet of lightweight cardboard
1 Popsicle stick
1 rubber band
masking tape

1. Cut a piece of cardboard to fit the two toilet paper tubes, which are the wheels of your catapult. Tape the cardboard to the wheels.

2. Cut a 2" x 2" piece of cardboard. Fold it in half. Then make a knot in one end of the rubber band. Cut a small hole in one side of the folded cardboard and pull it through. Tape the side without the rubber band firmly to the catapult body.

3. Now tape the Popsicle stick to the upper side of the cardboard as shown in the picture. Next, tape the other end of the rubber band tightly to the body of your catapult so that the rubber band is now 1" long.

4. Tape a 1" square piece of cardboard to the top of the Popsicle stick. Then use a dried bean to try out your catapult.

1.

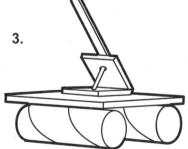

2.

3.

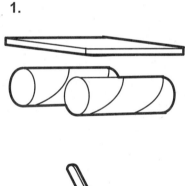

4.

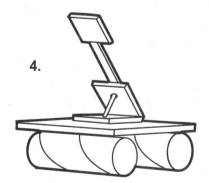

Lesson Assessment

Building a Castle

1. What were the first castles built of?

2. Let's look at this picture of a castle. Where is the moat? Where is the drawbridge?

3. Why did builders put moats around castles?

4. Why did enemies have to lay siege to a stone castle for months or even years at a time?

Student Guide
Lesson 3: Life in a Castle

Castles were the grandest of all medieval European homes. Hundreds of people lived and worked in a castle's many rooms and workspaces.

Lesson Objectives

- Demonstrate mastery of important knowledge and skills taught in previous lessons.
- Identify some of the people who lived or worked in a castle.
- Explain that castle life centered on the great hall.
- Explain that a castle was both a home and a fortress.

PREPARE

Approximate lesson time is 60 minutes.

Materials

For the Student
Optional

- Castle Life activity sheet
- Feasting in the Great Hall activity sheet
- Great Hall Diorama activity sheet
  pencils, no. 2
  paper, 8 1/2" x 11"
  pencils, colored, 16 or more
  paper, colored construction, 12"x12"
  paper, heavy
  Elmer's Glue-All
  scissors, round-end safety
  shoeboxes
  tape, clear
  A Medieval Feast by Aliki
  Life in a Medieval Castle and Village Coloring Book by John Green
  Living in Castle Times by Robyn Gee

Keywords and Pronunciation

drawbridge : A bridge that can be raised to prevent access or to permit a boat or ship to pass beneath it.

medieval (meh-DEE-vuhl) : Having to do with the Middle Ages.

moat : A deep wide ditch, usually filled with water, which surrounds a building.

scullion (SKUHL-yuhn)

siege (seej)

LEARN

Activity 1: Castle Facts *(Online)*

Activity 2: Visit a Castle *(Online)*

Activity 3: Show You Know *(Online)*

Activity 4: History Record Book *(Online)*

Activity 5. Optional: Life in a Castle *(Online)*

Activity 6. Optional: Feasting in the Great Hall *(Online)*

Activity 7. Optional: Make a Great Hall Diorama *(Online)*

ASSESS

Lesson Assessment: Life in a Castle (*Online*)

You will complete an offline assessment covering the main objectives of this lesson. Your learning coach will score this assessment.

LEARN

Activity 8. Optional: Read On! *(Online)*

Great Hall Diorama

cut

Name _____   Date _____

Castle Life Activity Sheet

Identify the roles of people in a medieval castle according to the following colors. Circle castle protectors in red. Circle entertainers in blue. Circle cooks and helpers in green. Circle the lord and his family in orange.

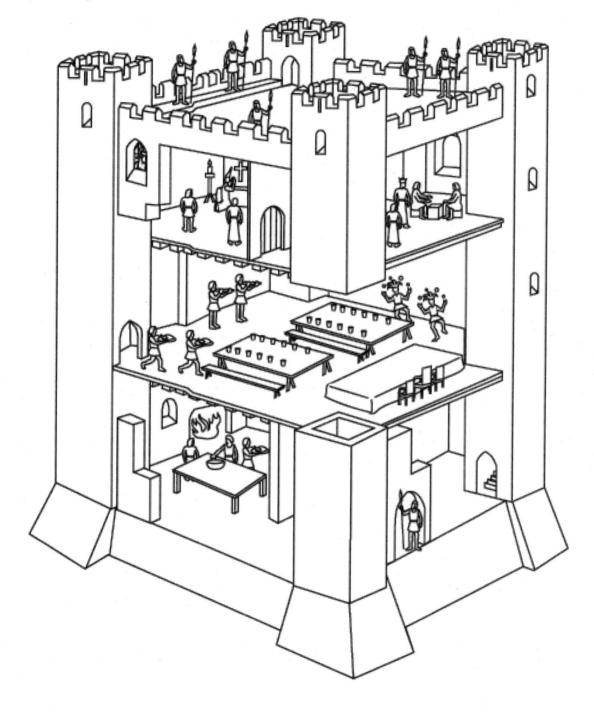

Name _____   **Date** _____

Feasting in the Great Hall

Color all of the details in the great hall, including the tapestries, the entertainers, the guests, and the feast. Write a caption in the box describing what is happening in the great hall.

Lesson Assessment

Life in a Castle

1. A castle wasn't only a fortress to defend against enemies. What other purposes did it have?

2. Who were some of the people who lived or worked in a castle?

3. Let's match up names to the pictures. Which of these is the lord of the castle? The scullion from the kitchen? The minstrel? The jester?

4. What was the name of the castle's main room where much activity took place and the feasts were held?

Student Guide
Lesson 4: What Is Knighthood?

Knights were armor-clad mounted warriors of the Middle Ages. The knightly code of honor is called the Code of Chivalry.

Lesson Objectives
- Demonstrate mastery of important knowledge and skills taught in previous lessons.
- Explain how knights used armor, lances, and swords.
- Identify the Code of Chivalry as a set of rules for knights' good behavior.
- Explain that knights served kings, queens, and lords by fighting their enemies.

PREPARE

Approximate lesson time is 60 minutes.

Materials
For the Student
> 🖳 *Knights in Shining Armor* question sheet

Optional
> 🖳 Knight in Shining Armor activity sheet
> 🖳 Knights in Shining Armor question sheet
>
> Knights in Shining Armor by Gail Gibbons
> pencils, no. 2
> paper, 8 1/2" x 11"
> pencils, colored, 16 or more
> markers, colored, 8 or more
> crayons, 16 or more
> paper, heavy
> Design Your Own Coat of Arms by Rosemary Chorzempa
> Knight in Armor Sticker Soldier (Dover Little Activity Books) by A. G. Smith
> Knights and Armor Coloring Book by A. G. Smith
> The Ultimate Castle and Knight Sticker Book by Deni Brown

Keywords and Pronunciation
chivalry (SHIH-vuhl-ree) : The actions of an ideal knight.

LEARN
Activity 1: Medieval Castles *(Online)*

Activity 2: Knights in Shining Armor *(Online)*

Activity 3: Show You Know *(Online)*

Activity 4: History Record Book *(Online)*

Activity 5. Optional: A Knight in Shining Armor *(Online)*

Activity 6. Optional: Create a Code of Chivalry *(Online)*

ASSESS

Lesson Assessment: What Is Knighthood? (*Online*)

You will complete an offline assessment covering the main objectives of this lesson. Your learning coach will score this assessment.

LEARN

Activity 7. Optional: Read On! *(Online)*

Knights in Shining Armor Discussion Questions

After reading page 3, ask the questions:
In feudal times, what work did a knight do for the ruler?
What did the ruler give to the knight in exchange?

A knight fought the ruler's enemies. The ruler gave the knight land and the right to rule over the peasants.

After reading page 5, have the child:
Point out the towers, moat, drawbridge, gates, courtyard, stables, and well.
(Look closely to find the well!)

After reading the first paragraph on page 8, ask the question:
If a squire named James became a knight, what would he be called?

Sir James

After reading page 11, have the child:
Find a shield and a lance and explain how knights used these. Point to your favorite coat of arms.

After reading page 15, look at the picture and then have the child:
Identify a sword, shield, and helmet.

Tell the child that a squire took an hour to help a knight put his armor on! Then ask the questions:
What is the differences between the two types of armor? Which armor do you think would be better protection?

One had rings called chain mail, and the other was made of metal plates.

After reading page 21, ask the question:
What was the purpose of a tournament?

It was a place for knights to test their skills.

After reading page 23, ask the question:
What were the rules of good behavior for a knight called?

the Code of Chivalry

After reading page 25, ask the question:
What happened to a knight if he broke the Code of Chivalry and did something bad?

The lord broke his sword and his spurs, and he wasn't allowed to be a knight anymore.

Name _____ **Date** _____

Knight in Shining Armor

Think of a name for your knight and write it in the box below. Then label your knight's equipment: sword, lance, helmet, and shield. Add a design to the shield. Then color this page. Now write a short story on the back telling how your knight got his equipment.

Sir

Name _____ Date _____

Lesson Assessment

What Is Knighthood?

1. What people did the knights serve, and how did they serve them?

2. Point to a sword and a lance in this image. How did a knight use these?

3. Why did knights wear armor?

4. What was the name for rules of good behavior that knights were supposed to follow?

Student Guide
Lesson 5: A Famous Knight: St. George and the Dragon

Chivalrous knights and their heroic deeds have been the subjects of epic tales and minstrels' songs since medieval times. Our story today tells of the legendary warrior St. George and his fight with a dragon.

Lesson Objectives

- Demonstrate mastery of important knowledge and skills taught in previous lessons.
- Name two of the following traits associated with heroic knights: they always fought bravely, they kept their promises, they helped those who needed it.
- Define *champion* as a person who fights or does great deeds for others.
- Explain that in the legend of Saint George, a brave knight defeats a dragon.

PREPARE

Approximate lesson time is 60 minutes.

Advance Preparation

- If you don't already have it, you will need the book *St. George and the Dragon* retold by Margaret Hodges and illustrated by Trina Schart Hyman (ISBN 316367958) for the activity in this lesson.

Materials

For the Student

    🖥 Saint George and the Dragon question sheet

Optional

    🖥 Knight Dice activity sheet

    St. George and the Dragon retold by Margaret Hodges and illustrated by Trina Schart Hyman

    pencils, no. 2

    paper, 8 1/2" x 11"

    pencils, colored, 16 or more

    bags, brown paper grocery

    paper, colored construction, 12"x12"

    Elmer's Glue-All

    glitter - gold

    markers, colored, 8 or more

    scissors, round-end safety

    tape, clear

    The Knight and the Dragon by Tomie dePaola

    The Reluctant Dragon by Kenneth Grahame

Keywords and Pronunciation

champion : A brave person who fights and does good deeds for others.

LEARN
Activity 1: Medieval Knights (Online)

Activity 2: Saint George and the Dragon (Online)

Activity 3: Show You Know (Online)

Activity 4: History Record Book (Online)

Activity 5. Optional: Make a Dragon (Online)

Activity 6. Optional: Knight Dice (Online)

ASSESS
Lesson Assessment: A Famous Knight: St. George and the Dragon (Online)
You will complete an offline assessment covering the main objectives of this lesson. Your learning coach will score this assessment.

LEARN
Activity 7. Optional: More Dragons (Online)

Saint George and the Dragon Discussion Questions

After reading page 7, tell the child:
Look at the picture and describe how the knight is dressed.

He's wearing armor with a sword, lance, and shield.

After reading page 8:
Briefly discuss the word *champion* (used in the first paragraph). Explain that the Red Cross Knight was not from Una's land. He was a champion, or a brave person who fights and does good deeds for others.

After reading page 12, discuss the following and ask the questions:
Knights are always supposed to help those in need.
Who needs help from the Red Cross Knight?

Una and her people

What deed will the knight have to do?

face the dragon

After reading page 19, discuss the following and ask the questions:
Knights were always supposed to be brave in battle. Do you think this knight is brave, and why? What do you think will happen next?

After reading page 27, tell the child:
St. George is now the village people's champion. A champion is a brave person who fights and does good deeds for others.

After reading page 31, discuss the following and ask the question:
The knight has made a promise to the Fairy Queen, and knights were always supposed to keep their promises. What has the knight promised the Fairy Queen?

to serve her for six years

The Knight Dice

Cut out the T-shaped figure. Fold it along the dotted lines. Tape them together to form a cube.

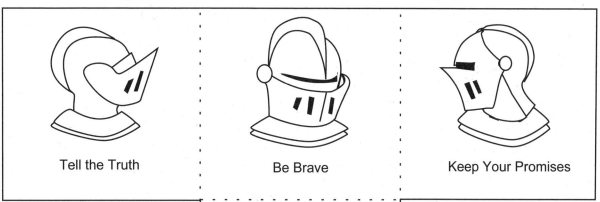

Tell the Truth   Be Brave   Keep Your Promises

Help Protect the Weak

Do Good Deeds for Others

Obey the Code of Chivalry

Lesson Assessment

A Famous Knight: St. George and the Dragon

1. What were some of the ways that knights were supposed to act?

2. What does the word *champion* mean?

3. In the story we read, what brave deed did Saint George do?

Student Guide
Lesson 6: Supposing You Were a Serf

Serfs made up the majority of the population in Europe in the Middle Ages. They were peasants who worked the land for the nobles, struggling to support their families. They had little freedom. They could be bought and sold with the land, but the lords had to protect them in time of attack.

Lesson Objectives
- Define *serf* as a peasant who served a noble (lord) by farming the land in exchange for protection.
- Describe the life of a serf as difficult and hard.
- Tell that serfs did not have freedom.

PREPARE

Approximate lesson time is 60 minutes.

Materials

    For the Student

    Optional

        📖 Who Am I? Flash Cards

        globe, inflatable

        pencils, no. 2

        paper, 8 1/2" x 11"

        pencils, colored, 16 or more

        bags, brown paper grocery

        cardboard, sheets

        paper, colored construction, 12"x12" - brown

        sand - about 3 cops

        bowl

        scissors, round-end safety

        string - about 24"

        toothpicks - 25

        water - about 4 cups

        The Duke and the Peasant: Life in the Middle Ages by Sister Wendy Beckett

Keywords and Pronunciation

Henri (ahn-REE)

Lord de Guise (deh GEEZ)

Marguerite (mahr-guh-REET)

serf : A peasant who served a noble by farming the land in exchange for protection.

LEARN
Activity 1: Feudalism Review *(Online)*

Activity 2: A Serf Forever? *(Online)*

Activity 3: Show You Know *(Online)*

Activity 4: History Record Book *(Online)*

Activity 5. Optional: Home Sweet Hovel *(Online)*

Activity 6. Optional: Who Am I? *(Online)*

ASSESS

Lesson Assessment: Supposing You Were a Serf (*Online*)
You will complete an offline assessment covering the main objectives of this lesson. Your learning coach will score this assessment.

LEARN
Activity 7. Optional: Rich and Poor *(Online)*

Who Am I? Flash Cards

Cut each Who Am I? flash card along the dotted lines and fold along the solid line. Shuffle the flash
cards and read the clue from side two. Guess whom the clue describes—a serf or a noble.

Noble	Noble	Noble
FOLD		
I give protection to the people who live on my land. Who am I?	I am the owner of land. Who am I?	I am also called "lord." Who am I?

Serf	Serf	Serf
FOLD		
I farm the land that is owned by the lord of my village. Who am I?	I am not free to leave my job when I want. Who am I?	I live a very hard life. Who am I?

Lesson Assessment

Supposing You Were a Serf

1. What was a serf?

2. Were the serfs free to leave the land whenever they wanted, or did they have to stay and work the noble's land?

3. What kind of life did serfs have?

Student Guide
Lesson 7: Building a Cathedral

Lesson Objectives

- Demonstrate mastery of important knowledge and skills taught in previous lessons.
- Identify the following features of a cathedral from pictures: spire, stained glass window, and stone sculptures.
- Define a cathedral as a large, important church.
- Explain that it took many years to build a cathedral.

PREPARE

Approximate lesson time is 60 minutes.

Materials

For the Student
Optional

  🖳 Cathedral Design activity sheet

  pencils, no. 2

  paper, 8 1/2" x 11"

  pencils, colored, 16 or more

  paper, colored construction, 12"x12" - black

  tissue paper - different colors (5)

  Elmer's Glue-All

  paper, wax

  scissors, round-end safety

  A Medieval Cathedral (Inside Story) by Fiona MacDonald

  Cathedral: The Story of Its Construction by David Macaulay

Keywords and Pronunciation

cathedral : A large important church.

Notre Dame (noh-truh DAHM)

LEARN
Activity 1: Reviewing Serfs and Nobles *(Online)*

Activity 2: Cathedral *(Online)*

Activity 3: Building Notre Dame *(Online)*

Activity 4: Show You Know *(Online)*

Activity 5: History Record Book *(Online)*

Activity 6. Optional: Cathedral Features *(Online)*

Activity 7. Optional: Rose Window *(Online)*

ASSESS

Lesson Assessment: Building a Cathedral (*Online*)

You will complete an offline assessment covering the main objectives of this lesson. Your learning coach will score this assessment.

LEARN

Activity 8. Optional: More on Cathedrals *(Online)*

Name _____   **Date** _____

Notre Dame Cathedral

Take a closer look at some of the unique features of a cathedral. Use the word bank to fill in the blanks to identify these features. Color the cathedral.

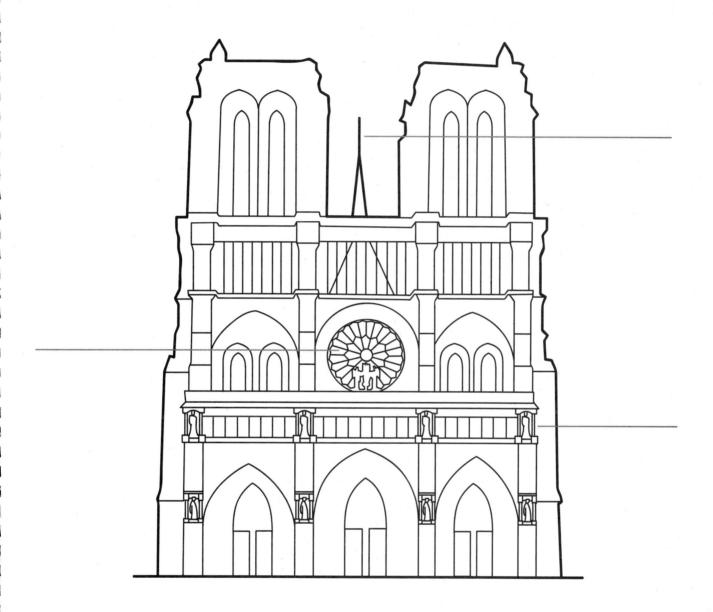

Word Bank

spire	stained-glass window	stone sculpture

Name _____   Date _____

Lesson Assessment

Building a Cathedral

1. What is a cathedral?

2. How long did it take to build a cathedral?

3. In this picture of a cathedral, show me a spire, stained glass windows, and a stone sculpture. (Hint: Look closely on either side of the large stained glass window and on the roof to find the stone sculptures.)

Student Guide
Lesson 8: Come to the Fair!

Cathedral cities were often sites for medieval fairs, where merchants from across Europe sold their wares, and people enjoyed jugglers, dancing, jousting, and more.

Lesson Objectives
- Demonstrate mastery of important knowledge and skills taught in previous lessons.
- Explain that fairs were often held in cathedral cities.
- Describe fairs as events at which merchants from all over Europe sold goods.
- Explain that fairs had many kinds of food and entertainment, such as musicians, acrobats, jousting knights, and dancers.

PREPARE

Approximate lesson time is 60 minutes.

Materials
For the Student
- 🖥 map of Medieval Europe, 1097-1300 A.D.

Optional
- 🖥 What Belongs? activity sheet
- pencils, no. 2
- paper, 8 1/2" x 11"
- pencils, colored, 16 or more
- cardboard, sheets - white
- markers, colored, 8 or more
- crayons, 16 or more

LEARN
Activity 1: Review What You Know *(Online)*

Activity 2: Pilgrimage *(Online)*

Activity 3: Come to the Fair! *(Online)*

Activity 4: Show You Know *(Online)*

Activity 5: History Record Book *(Online)*

Activity 6. Optional: Put It All Together in a Poster *(Online)*

Activity 7. Optional: What Belongs? *(Online)*

ASSESS

Lesson Assessment: Come to the Fair! (*Online*)

You will complete an offline assessment covering the main objectives of this lesson. Your learning coach will score this assessment.

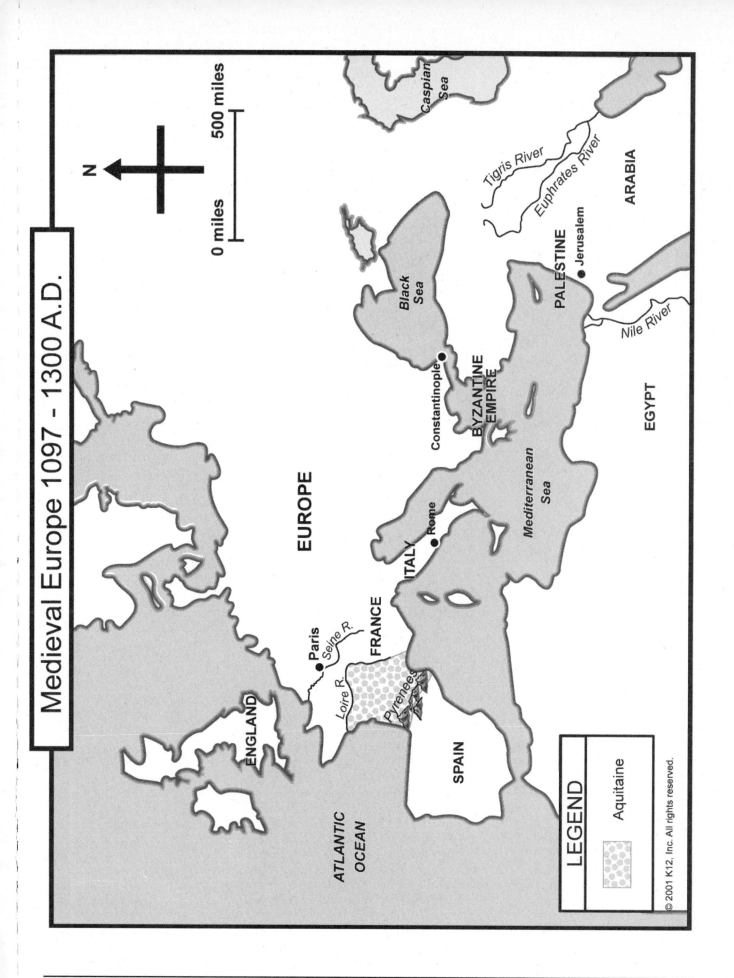

Medieval Europe 1097 – 1300 A.D.

N

500 miles

0 miles

EUROPE

ENGLAND

ATLANTIC OCEAN

Paris
Seine R.
Loire R.
FRANCE

Pyrenees

SPAIN

ITALY

Rome

Mediterranean Sea

Black Sea

Caspian Sea

Constantinople

BYZANTINE EMPIRE

PALESTINE
Jerusalem

Tigris River

Euphrates River

ARABIA

Nile River

EGYPT

LEGEND

Aquitaine

Name

Date

What Belongs?

Circle the pictures of things you would have seen at a medieval fair. Cross out the pictures that do not belong.

Name _____ Date _____

Lesson Assessment

Come to the Fair!

1. Why did merchants come to the fair?

2. Where did the merchants come from?

3. Besides rugs, wine, cloth and other things to buy, what else would you find at a fair?

4. Where were fairs often held?

Student Guide
Lesson 9: One in a Million: Eleanor of Aquitaine

Eleanor of Aquitaine was a spirited, independent woman who ruled as Queen of France and Queen of England. She came to be known as "The Grandmother of Europe."

Lesson Objectives

- Demonstrate mastery of important knowledge and skills taught in previous lessons.
- Explain that Eleanor of Aquitaine was the Queen of England and the Queen of France.
- Demonstrate mastery of important knowledge and skills in this unit.
- Define a cathedral as a large, important church.
- Identify feudalism as a system in which people exchanged land, loyalty, and service in return for protection.
- List the order of rule in feudalism: king, noble, knight, serf.
- Explain that stone castles were hard to attack.
- Explain that a castle was both a home and a fortress.
- Identify the Code of Chivalry as a set of rules for knights' good behavior.
- Explain that in the legend of Saint George, a brave knight defeats a dragon.
- Describe the life of a serf as difficult and hard.
- Explain that fairs had many kinds of food and entertainment, such as musicians, acrobats, jousting knights, and dancers.

PREPARE

Approximate lesson time is 60 minutes.

Materials

For the Student

    🖳 map of Medieval Europe 1097-1300 A.D.

    crayons, 16 or more

Optional

    🖳 Queen of Two Countries activity sheet

    pencils, no. 2

    markers, colored, 8 or more

    🖳 Queen's World activity sheet

Keywords and Pronunciation

Aquitaine (A-kwuh-tayn)

Loire (lwahr)

Pyrenees (PIR-uh-neez)

troubadours (TROO-buh-dohrz)

LEARN
Activity 1: Cathedral Review *(Online)*

Activity 2: Aquitaine *(Online)*

Activity 3: Queen Eleanor *(Online)*

Activity 4. Optional: Queen of Two Countries *(Online)*

Activity 5. Optional: The Queen's World *(Online)*

Activity 6: Unit Review: the Feudal World *(Online)*

ASSESS
Unit Assessment: The Feudal World *(Offline)*
Complete an offline Unit Assessment. Your learning coach will score this part of the Assessment.

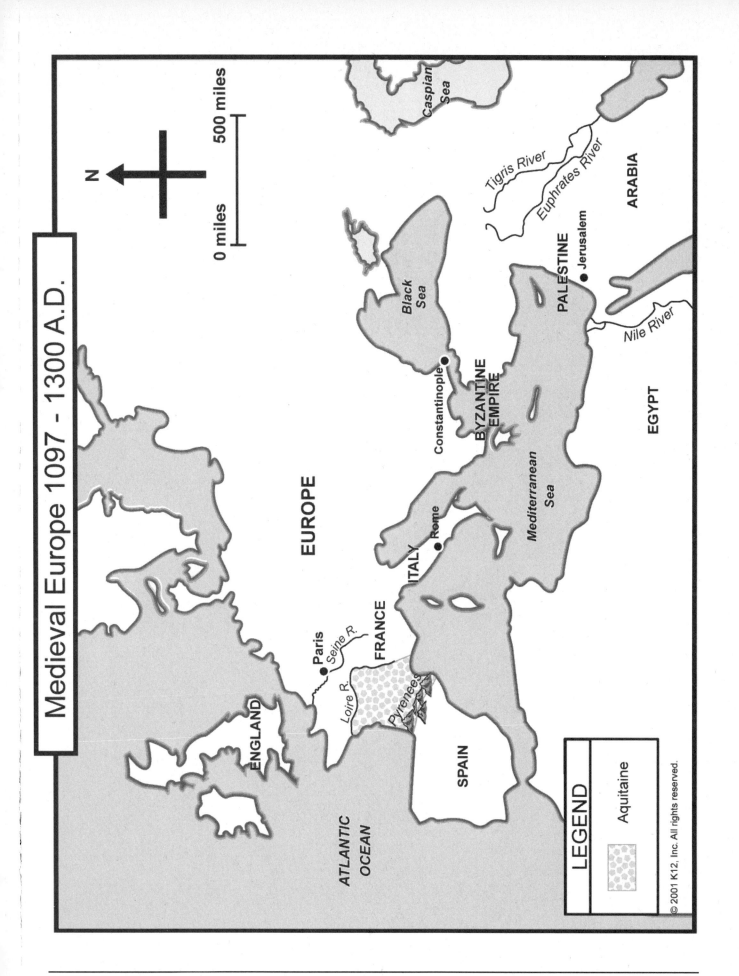

Medieval Europe 1097 – 1300 A.D.

500 miles

0 miles

N

Caspian Sea

Tigris River

Euphrates River

ARABIA

Black Sea

Palestine

Jerusalem

Constantinople

BYZANTINE EMPIRE

Nile River

EGYPT

EUROPE

Mediterranean Sea

Rome

ITALY

FRANCE

Paris

Seine R.

Loire R.

Pyrenees

ENGLAND

SPAIN

ATLANTIC OCEAN

LEGEND

Aquitaine

© 2001 K12, Inc. All rights reserved.

Name _____   Date _____

Queen of Two Countries

Eleanor of Aquitaine was the queen of two countries. Use markers to color in both countries and use your knowledge of this special person to answer the question at the bottom.

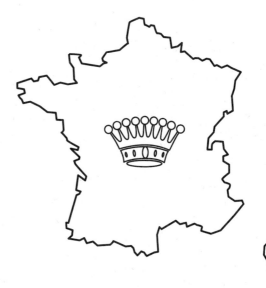

Eleanor of Aquitaine,
Queen of England

Eleanor of Aquitaine,
Queen of France

Why was Eleanor of Aquitaine such an important person in history?

_____

_____

_____

_____

Name _____   Date _____

Queen's World

Find the two countries Eleanor helped rule. Write the name of each country in the spaces provided on the activity sheet. Then draw a line from each name to the country on the activity sheet. Find and label Aquitaine, Eleanor's homeland.

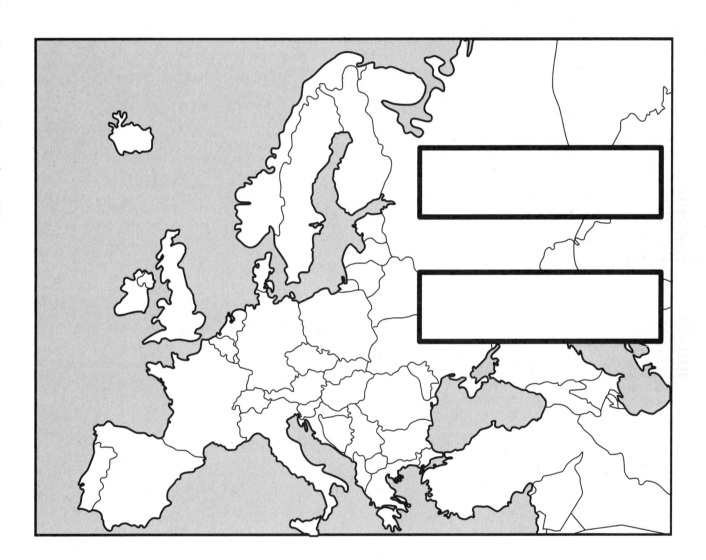

Name _____ Date _____

The Feudal World

Read each sentence and its answer choices. Fill in the bubble in front of the word or words that best answer the question.

1. Which of these shows the people listed in order from the most important to the least important, according to the order of rule in feudalism?
   - ○ king, knight, noble, serf
   - ○ serf, noble, king, knight
   - ○ king, noble, knight, serf

2. Feudalism meant that people exchanged land, loyalty, and service in return for what?
   - ○ protection
   - ○ education
   - ○ money

3. Which of the following is the name for a large, important church with a spire, stained glass windows, and stone sculptures?
   - ○ mosque
   - ○ cathedral
   - ○ monastery

4. Who followed a Code of Chivalry and used armor, lances, and swords?
   - ○ serfs
   - ○ knights
   - ○ nobles

5. Who farmed the land, were not free, and had a difficult life?
   - ○ serfs
   - ○ knights
   - ○ nobles

6. What took place at fairs in the Middle Ages?
   - ○ Bishops from western Europe built cathedrals.
   - ○ Sailors from the Mediterranean raced ships.
   - ○ Merchants from all over Europe sold goods.

7. What happened in the legend of Saint George?
   - ○ A hardworking serf defeated a dragon.
   - ○ A mean noble became a champion.
   - ○ A brave knight defeated a dragon.

8. What did a castle serve as?
   - ○ a tomb and a resting place
   - ○ a fortress and a home
   - ○ a home and a port

9. Why did armies lay siege to stone castles and use weapons such as catapults?
   - ○ Castles were hard to attack.
   - ○ The armies needed to practice.
   - ○ It was easy to get into the castles.

10. Eleanor of Aquitaine was queen of which two countries?
    - ○ Spain and France
    - ○ Italy and England
    - ○ England and France

Student Guide
Lesson 1: Command from the Pope

During the Crusades European Christians marched east to capture "the Holy Land" from Muslims. King Richard I led his English army against the Muslim leader, Saladin. In England the legendary Robin Hood helped the poor, and the Magna Carta guaranteed some English rights. England and France fought the Hundred Years War, and Joan of Arc came to the rescue.

Lesson Objectives
- Demonstrate mastery of important knowledge and skills taught in previous lessons.
- Explain that the Crusades were wars between European Christians and Muslims for possession of Palestine and especially for the city of Jerusalem.
- Explain that the crusaders wore a cross on their clothes.
- State that Palestine is called "the Holy Land."
- Identify Jerusalem as being sacred to Jews, Christians, and Muslims.

PREPARE

Approximate lesson time is 60 minutes.

Materials
For the Student
- map of Medieval Europe 1097-1300 A.D.
- map of the Islamic Empire, 750 - 900 A.D.

Optional
- Crusader's Helmet pattern
  pencils, no. 2
  paper, 8 1/2" x 11"
  pencils, colored, 16 or more
  glue sticks
  paper, colored construction, 12"x12" - purple and yellow (2)
  scissors, round-end safety
  yarn - yellow
  paint, gold - spray
  paper, colored construction, 12"x12" - white
  household items - plumes, X-Acto knife
  stapler

Keywords and Pronunciation
Palestine (PA-luh-stiyn)
Seljuk (sel-JOOK)

LEARN
Activity 1: Medieval Times *(Online)*

Activity 2: The Pope Speaks *(Online)*

Activity 3: Show You Know *(Online)*

Activity 4: History Record Book *(Online)*

Activity 5. Optional: Palestine: Important to All *(Online)*

Activity 6. Optional: Crusader's Helmet *(Online)*

ASSESS

Lesson Assessment: Command from the Pope (*Online*)

You will complete an offline assessment covering the main objectives of this lesson. Your learning coach will score this assessment.

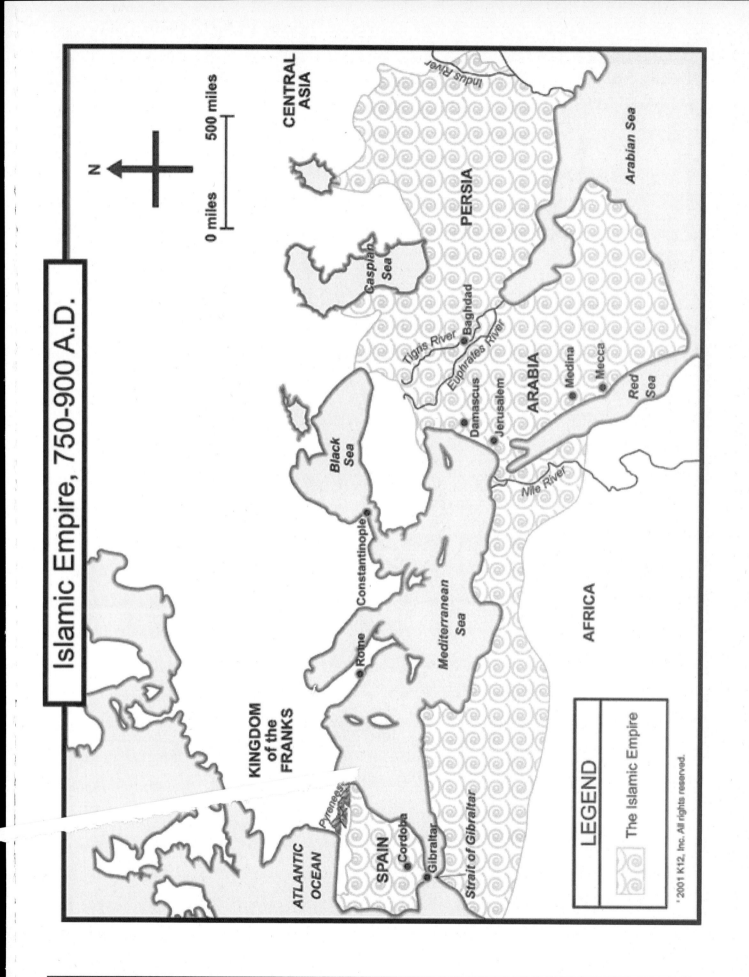

Islamic Empire, 750–900 A.D.

N

0 miles
500 miles

CENTRAL ASIA

Indus River

PERSIA

Arabian Sea

Caspian Sea

Tigris River
Baghdad
Euphrates River

Medina

Mecca

ARABIA

Red Sea

Damascus

Jerusalem

Black Sea

Nile River

Constantinople

Mediterranean Sea

AFRICA

Rome

KINGDOM of the FRANKS

Pyrenees

ATLANTIC OCEAN

SPAIN

Cordoba

Gibraltar

Strait of Gibraltar

LEGEND

The Islamic Empire

* 2001 K12, Inc. All rights reserved.

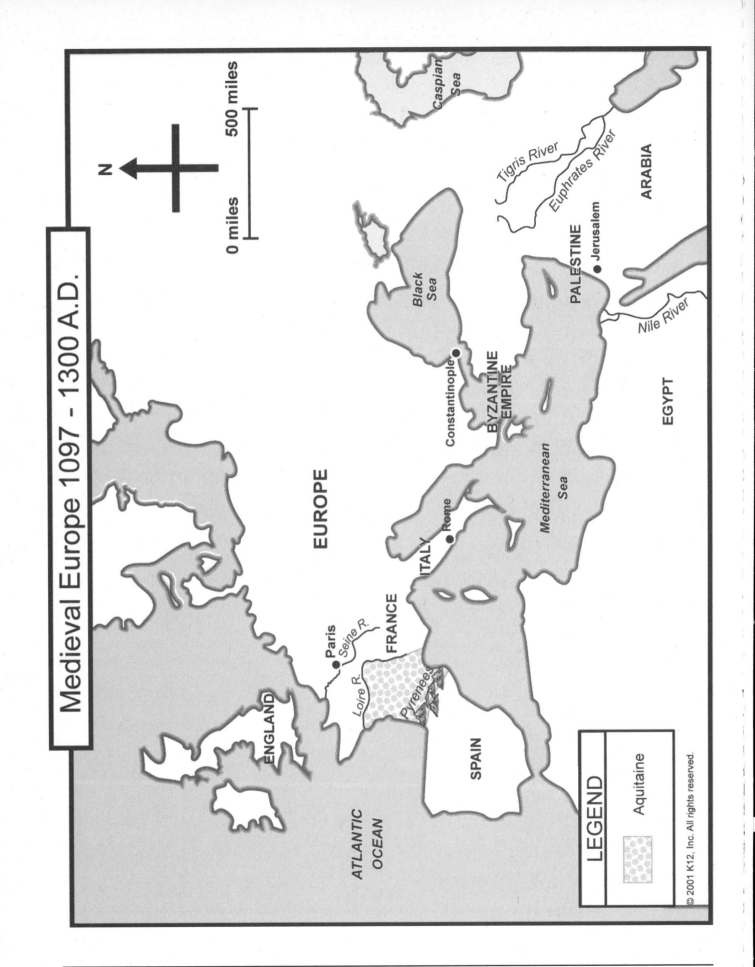

Medieval Europe 1097 – 1300 A.D.

N

500 miles

0 miles

EUROPE

ENGLAND

ATLANTIC
OCEAN

Paris
Seine R.
FRANCE
Loire R.
Pyrenees

SPAIN

ITALY
Rome

Mediterranean
Sea

Black
Sea

Constantinople

BYZANTINE
EMPIRE

Caspian
Sea

Tigris River

Euphrates River

ARABIA

PALESTINE
Jerusalem

Nile River

EGYPT

LEGEND

Aquitaine

© 2001 K12, Inc. All rights reserved.

Pattern for a Crusader's Helmet

Follow these directions to make a crusader's helmet.

1. Use the dimensions on the pattern to draw the helmet on the sheet of construction paper.

2. Cut out the helmet.

3. Cut along the top to make 1-inch strips.

4. Use a single-edged razor blade or X-Acto knife to cut out the design for the eyes and nose.

5. Staple the helmet along the 8.5-inch margin to make a cylinder.

6. Fold the 1-inch strips over in a gentle bend to the center, one atop the other, until all are folded into the center. Staple the ends of the strips together at the top.

7. Paint the helmet using gold or silver spray paint.

8. After it has dried, add plumes to the top of the helmet.

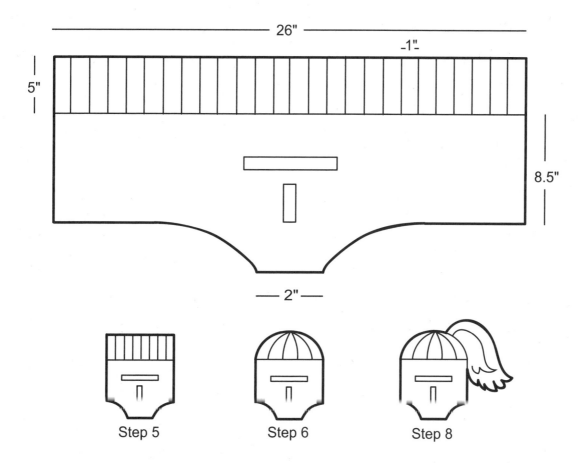

Step 5   Step 6   Step 8

Lesson Assessment

Command from the Pope

1. What was the name of the city in Palestine that was holy to Jews, Christians, and Muslims?

2. Because Palestine is sacred to Jews, Christians, and Muslims, what is another name for it?

3. What were the Crusades?

4. What land were the Christians and Muslims fighting for?

5. What did the crusaders wear on their clothes?

Student Guide
Lesson 2: Richard the Lion-Heart and Saladin

Lesson Objectives

- Demonstrate mastery of important knowledge and skills taught in previous lessons.
- Name Saladin as the leader of the Muslims during some of the Crusades.
- Name King Richard I of England as the "lion-hearted" warrior king.
- Explain that King Richard I and Saladin led armies against each other during some of the Crusades and then made a truce.

PREPARE

Approximate lesson time is 60 minutes.

Materials

For the Student

     map of Medieval Europe, 1097-1300 A.D.

     pencils, no. 2

     paper, 8 1/2" x 11"

     pencils, colored, 16 or more

Optional

     tablets, medium-lined handwriting

     Crusades: The Struggle for the Holy Lands by Chris Rice and Peter Dennis

Keywords and Pronunciation

Palestine (PA-luh-stiyn)

Saladin (SAL-uh-din)

Seljuk (sel-JOOK)

LEARN
Activity 1: Review the Crusades *(Online)*

Activity 2: Saladin *(Online)*

Activity 3: Saladin and King Richard the Lion-Heart *(Online)*

Activity 4: Results of the Crusades *(Online)*

Activity 5: Show You Know *(Online)*

Activity 6: History Record Book *(Online)*

Activity 7. Optional: The Ballad of Richard and Saladin *(Online)*

Activity 8. Optional: The Truce *(Online)*

ASSESS

Lesson Assessment: Richard the Lion-Heart and Saladin (*Online*)

You will complete an offline assessment covering the main objectives of this lesson. Your learning coach will score this assessment.

LEARN

Activity 9. Optional: Struggle for the Holy Lands *(Online)*

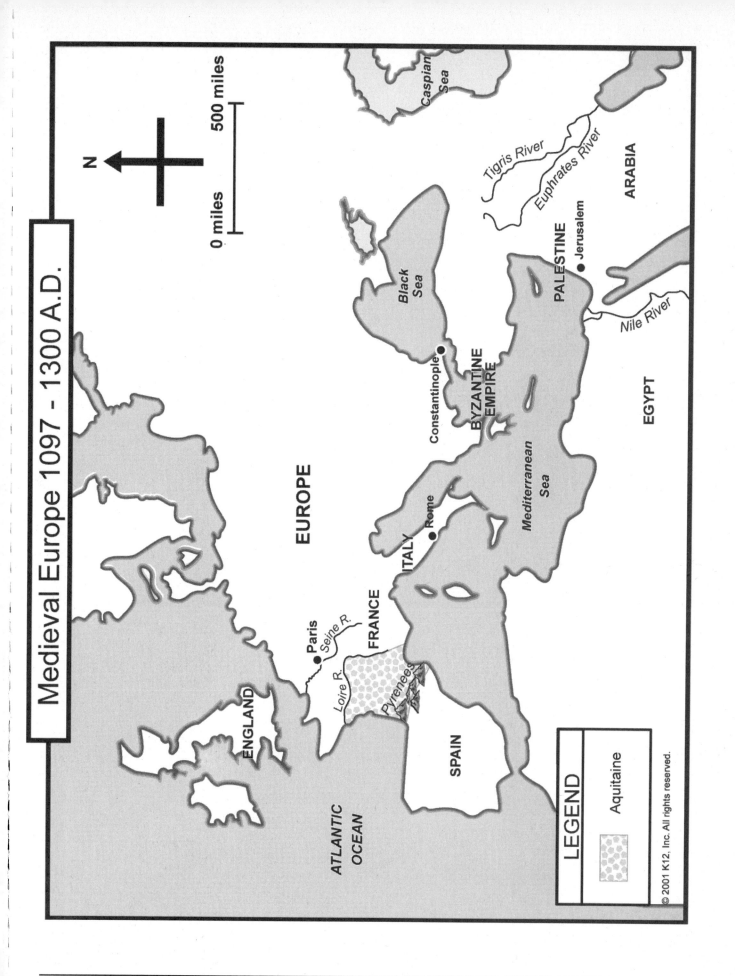

Medieval Europe 1097 – 1300 A.D.

N

500 miles

0 miles

Caspian Sea

Tigris River

Euphrates River

ARABIA

Jerusalem

PALESTINE

Black Sea

Nile River

Constantinople

BYZANTINE EMPIRE

EGYPT

EUROPE

Mediterranean Sea

Rome

ITALY

FRANCE

Paris

Seine R.

Loire R.

Pyrenees

ENGLAND

SPAIN

ATLANTIC OCEAN

LEGEND

Aquitaine

© 2001 K12, Inc. All rights reserved.

153

Lesson Assessment

Richard the Lion-Heart and Saladin

1. Who was the leader of the Muslim armies during some of the Crusades?

2. Who was the "lion-hearted" warrior king from England who fought in some of the Crusades?

3. Explain what King Richard I and Saladin did.

Student Guide
Lesson 3: The Legend of Robin Hood

Lesson Objectives

- Demonstrate mastery of important knowledge and skills taught in previous lessons.
- Name Robin Hood as the legendary English outlaw who stole from the rich and gave to the poor.
- State that Robin Hood lived in Sherwood Forest.
- Explain the Robin Hood met Little John when they fought on a footbridge.

PREPARE

Approximate lesson time is 60 minutes.

Materials

For the Student

> pencils, no. 2
>
> paper, 8 1/2" x 11"
>
> pencils, colored, 16 or more

Optional

> bag, brown paper, lunch
>
> cardboard, boxes
>
> cardboard, sheets
>
> clay, colored
>
> foil, aluminum
>
> leaf - several
>
> paper, colored construction, 12"x12" - white, blue, green, brown
>
> twig - several
>
> Elmer's Glue-All
>
> scissors, round-end safety
>
> shoeboxes
>
> tablets, medium-lined handwriting
>
> Robin Hood by Annie Ingle
>
> The Adventures of Robin Hood by Marcia Williams
>
> The Merry Adventures of Robin Hood by Howard Pyle

Keywords and Pronunciation

Palestine (PA-luh-stiyn)

Seljuk (sel-JOOK)

LEARN
Activity 1: Richard and Saladin *(Online)*

Activity 2: Robin Hood Meets Little John *(Online)*

Activity 3: Show You Know *(Online)*

Activity 4: History Record Book *(Online)*

Activity 5. Optional: Robin Hood Versus Little John *(Online)*

Activity 6. Optional: A Letter Home *(Online)*

ASSESS
Lesson Assessment: The Legend of Robin Hood *(Online)*
You will complete an offline assessment covering the main objectives of this lesson. Your learning coach will score this assessment.

LEARN
Activity 7. Optional: More Adventures of Robin Hood *(Online)*

Lesson Assessment

The Legend of Robin Hood

1. According to legend, who is the English outlaw who stole from the rich and gave to the poor?

2. Where did Robin Hood live?

3. How did Robin Hood meet Little John?

Student Guide
Lesson 4: King John and the Magna Carta

Lesson Objectives
- Demonstrate mastery of important knowledge and skills taught in previous lessons.
- Identify King John as a king of England.
- Identify 1215 as the year the Magna Carta was signed.
- Define the Magna Carta as a guarantee of rights that even the king had to obey.

PREPARE

Approximate lesson time is 60 minutes.

Materials
For the Student

    pencils, no. 2

    paper, 8 1/2" x 11"

    pencils, colored, 16 or more

Optional

    🖳 Magna Carta activity sheet

    🖳 Magna Carta Skit activity sheet

    pens

Keywords and Pronunciation
Palestine (PA-luh-stiyn)

Runnymede (RUH-nee-meed)

Seljuk (sel-JOOK)

Thames (temz)

LEARN
Activity 1: Review *(Online)*

Activity 2: The Magna Carta *(Online)*

Activity 3: Show You Know *(Online)*

Activity 4: History Record Book (Online)

Activity 5. Optional: Magna Carta: Document of Documents (Online)

Activity 6. Optional: Dialogue with King John (Online)

ASSESS

Lesson Assessment: King John and the Magna Carta (Online)

You will complete an offline assessment covering the main objectives of this lesson. Your learning coach will score this assessment.

Name _____ Date _____

The Magna Carta

Fill in each blank with the correct word.

Magna Carta

The Magna Carta was signed in _____. The

English nobles forced King _____ to sign

the paper. This great charter said the king had to

obey the _____ of the land. The agreement

also gave certain rights to people. One right was

that people could not be punished unless given a

fair _____.

Signing of the Magna Carta

Setting: Runnymede, England—1215

The setting is a meadow in early summer. Tents have been pitched, colorful banners wave in the fresh breeze, and horses graze in a roped off area behind the tents. Most of the important nobles in England have come to Runnymede for this historic occasion. Also present are bishops and archbishops of the church.

King John sits upon a make-shift wooden throne under a pavilion. A small table sits on the ground in front him. Around him stand the many nobles that have grown tired of King John's demands. They are forcing him to accept and sign the "grand charter", or agreement, they have written.

This charter will force the king to follow the laws. It will also give certain rights to the nobles. It is truly an historic occasion.

Lord William (Bows toward, then addresses King John): John, King of England, the noblemen have asked me to speak.

King John: You may speak, Lord William.

Lord William: The nobles are tired of you taking our money whenever you want. We are tired of being thrown into prison. We are tired of sending you our knights whenever you go to war.

King John (Stands and speaks to everyone): I am the king of England! Everyone must do what I say.

Lord William: We disagree. There should be limits to the power of a king. You should not be able to do anything you want.

King John (Sits): And how, Lord William, will you make sure that I will not do whatever I want?

Signing of the Magna Carta

Lord William: The nobles of England have written a charter. You will sign this agreement, as will the nobles. By signing the Magna Carta, you will promise to obey the law and give the nobles certain rights. Future kings will also have to follow the Magna Carta.

Lord William approaches the table, sets the charter and a pen on it, and withdraws a couple of steps, bowing.

King John looks around and sees the determined looks on the nobles' faces. He realizes he has no choice but to sign the charter.

Reluctantly, he picks up the pen and signs his name at the bottom, the presses his ring into the soft wax. This makes the document official.

King John (Stands and speaks to everyone): Barons, earls, lords, knights, and bishops of England—I have affixed my seal to the Magna Carta.

The nobles cheer loudly their approval and celebrate their victory over King John.

Name _____ Date _____

Lesson Assessment

King John and the Magna Carta

1. Of what country was John the king?

2. Name two things the Magna Carta said.

3. In what year was the Magna Carta signed?

Student Guide
Lesson 5: The Hundred Years' War

Lesson Objectives
- Demonstrate mastery of important knowledge and skills taught in previous lessons.
- Name England and France as the two countries that fought the Hundred Years' War.
- Explain that the Hundred Years' War was fought for control of France.
- Name the longbow and the cannon as two weapons introduced during the Hundred Years' War.

PREPARE

Approximate lesson time is 60 minutes.

Materials
For the Student

    📖 map of England and France

Optional

    📖 Hundred Years War activity sheet

    pencils, no. 2

    paper, 8 1/2" x 11"

    pencils, colored, 16 or more

    tablets, medium-lined handwriting

    yarn

Keywords and Pronunciation
Palestine (PA-luh-stiyn)
Seljuk (sel-JOOK)

LEARN
Activity 1: A Review *(Online)*

Activity 2: A Hundred Years of Fighting *(Online)*

Activity 3: Show You Know *(Online)*

Activity 4: History Record Book *(Online)*

Activity 5. Optional: Letter Home (Online)

Activity 6. Optional: The English Versus The French (Online)

ASSESS

Lesson Assessment: The Hundred Years' War (Online)

You will complete an offline assessment covering the main objectives of this lesson. Your learning coach will score this assessment.

LEARN

Activity 7. Optional: Rosemary the Preservative (Online)

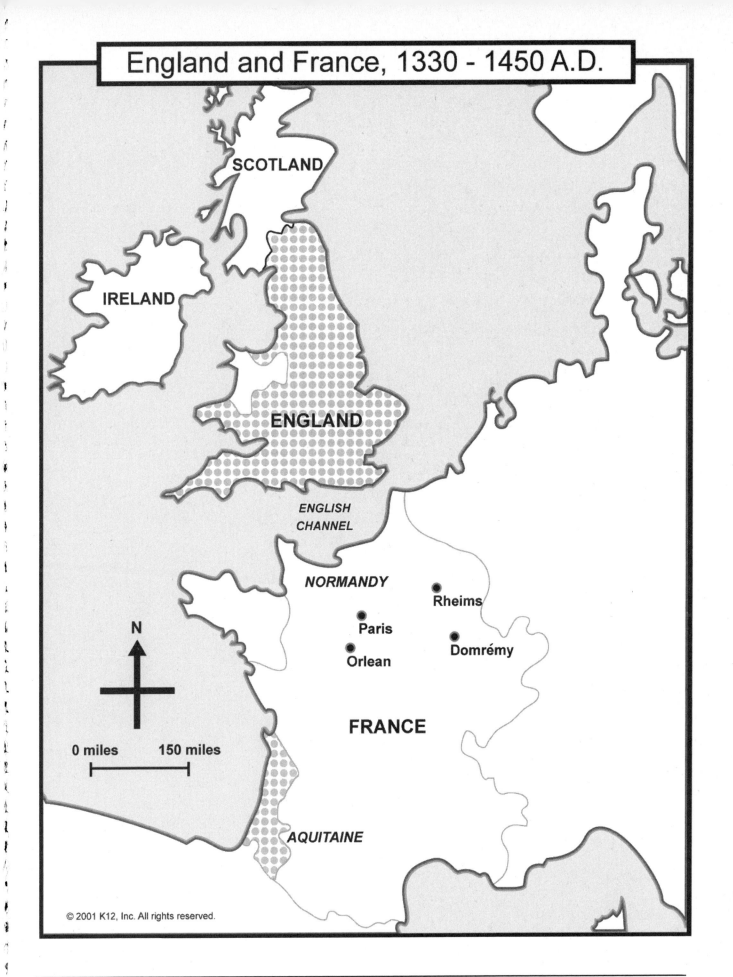

England and France, 1330 - 1450 A.D.

SCOTLAND

IRELAND

ENGLAND

ENGLISH CHANNEL

NORMANDY

Rheims

Paris

Domrémy

Orlean

N

0 miles   150 miles

FRANCE

AQUITAINE

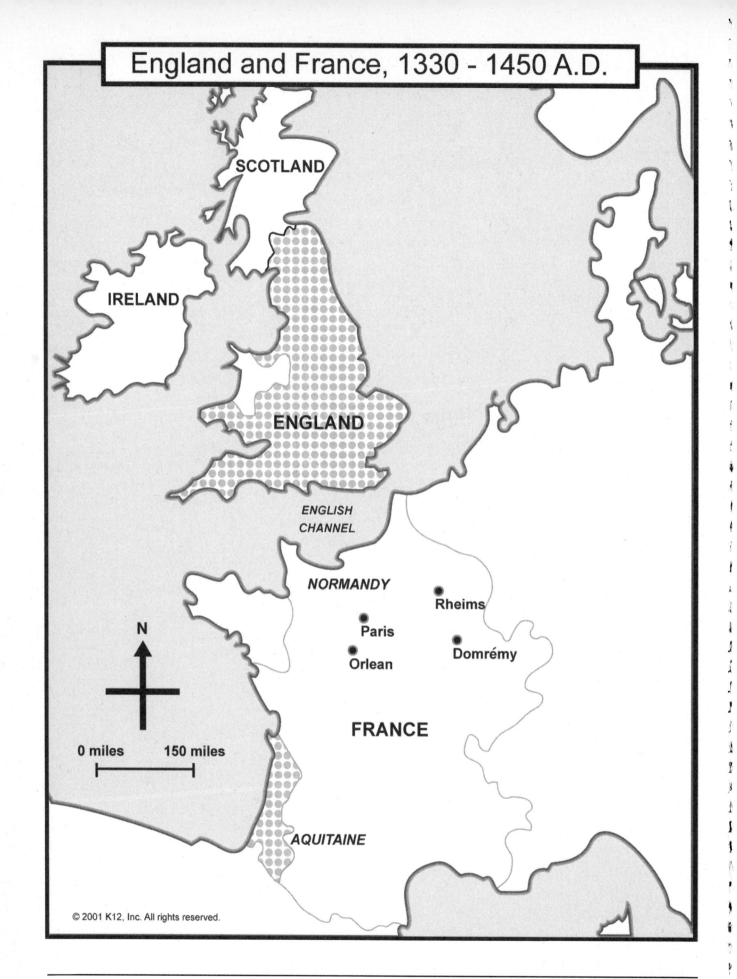

England and France, 1330 - 1450 A.D.

SCOTLAND

IRELAND

ENGLAND

ENGLISH CHANNEL

NORMANDY

Rheims

Paris

Orlean

Domrémy

N

0 miles   150 miles

FRANCE

AQUITAINE

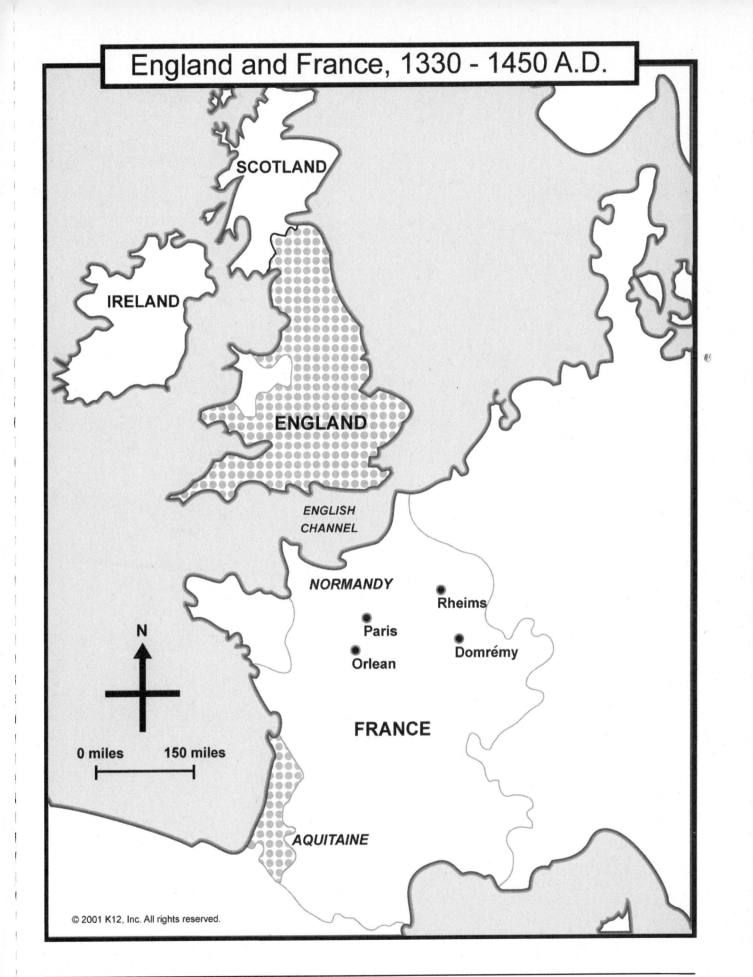

England and France, 1330 - 1450 A.D.

SCOTLAND

IRELAND

ENGLAND

ENGLISH CHANNEL

NORMANDY

Rheims

Paris

Orlean

Domrémy

N

0 miles   150 miles

FRANCE

AQUITAINE

Name _____ Date _____

The Hundred Years War

1. Write the words "England" and "France" in the correct blanks below.
2. Draw one of each of the following symbols below the name of the country that introduced these weapons in this war.

3. This war was fought for control over what country? Color part of this country green.
4. Which country won the war? Draw a circle around the name of this country.
5. Color part of the English Channel blue.

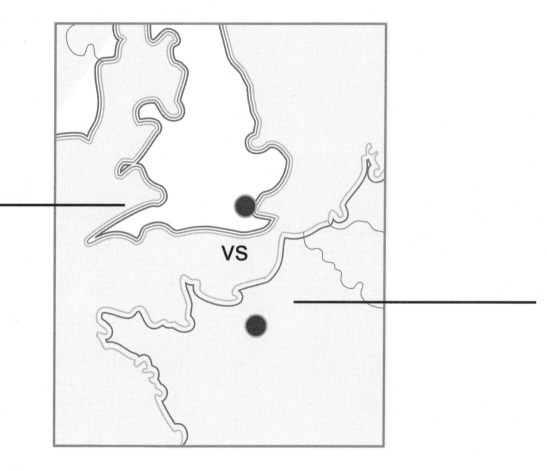

Name _____   Date _____

Lesson Assessment

The Hundred Years' War

1. What two countries fought against each other in the Hundred Years' War?

2. Why were the two countries fighting the Hundred Years' War?

3. The English introduced two weapons during the Hundred Years' War. What were they?

Student Guide
Lesson 6: Joan of Arc: The Girl Who Saved France

Lesson Objectives

- Demonstrate mastery of important knowledge and skills taught in previous lessons.
- Explain that Joan of Arc led the French against the English during the end of the Hundred Years' War.
- Explain that Joan of Arc said she had visions telling her to lead the French army.
- State that France won the Hundred Years' War.

PREPARE

Approximate lesson time is 60 minutes.

Materials

For the Student

- map of England and France

Optional

- Joan of Arc activity sheet

  pencils, no. 2

  paper, 8 1/2" x 11"

  pencils, colored, 16 or more

  paper, colored construction, 12"x12" - white (2)

  markers, colored, 8 or more

  Joan of Arc by Diane Stanley

  Joan of Arc by Josephine Poole

  Joan of Arc: The Lily Maid by Margaret Hodges

Keywords and Pronunciation

D'Arc (dahrk)
Domrémy (dohn-ray-MEE)
Orléans (or-lay-AHN)
Palestine (PA-luh-stiyn)
Rheims (reems)
Seljuk (sel-JOOK)

LEARN
Activity 1: Review: Hundred Years' War *(Online)*

Activity 2: Joan's Vision *(Online)*

Activity 3: Show You Know *(Online)*

Activity 4: History Record Book *(Online)*

Activity 5. Optional: Joan's Banner *(Online)*

Activity 6. Optional: Joan of Arc *(Online)*

ASSESS

Lesson Assessment: Joan of Arc: The Girl Who Saved France *(Online)*

You will complete an offline assessment covering the main objectives of this lesson. Your learning coach will score this assessment.

LEARN
Activity 7. Optional: Read More About Joan of Arc *(Online)*

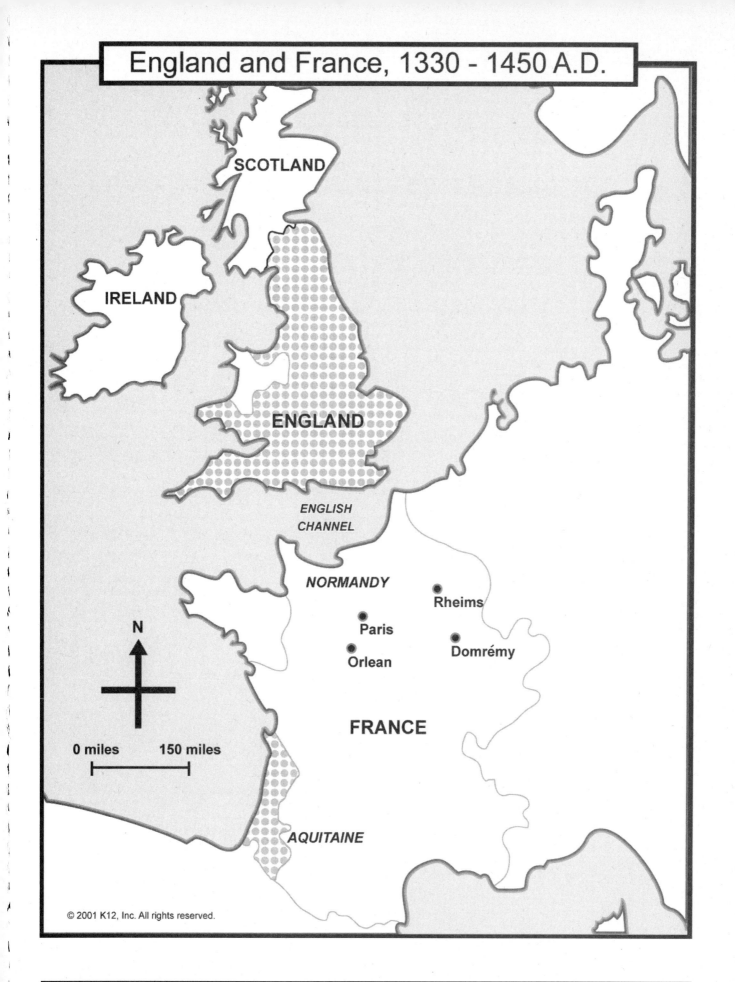

England and France, 1330 - 1450 A.D.

SCOTLAND

IRELAND

ENGLAND

ENGLISH CHANNEL

NORMANDY

Rheims

Paris

Orlean

Domrémy

N

FRANCE

0 miles   150 miles

AQUITAINE

Lesson Assessment

Joan of Arc: The Girl Who Saved France

1. Who did Joan of Arc lead against the English during the end of the Hundred Years' War?

2. Joan of Arc decided to lead the French forces into battle. According to Joan, what had told her to do this?

3. Who won the Hundred Years' War?

Student Guide
Lesson 7: Towns and Trade

Lesson Objectives

- Demonstrate mastery of important knowledge and skills taught in previous lessons.
- Explain that medieval towns became centers of trade and craftsmanship.
- Explain that medieval towns grew as people arrived to sell their products.
- Describe two characteristics of medieval towns, such as they had lots of shops and narrow twisting streets.

PREPARE

Approximate lesson time is 60 minutes.

Materials

For the Student
Optional
- 🖥 Growing Towns activity sheet
  pencils, no. 2
  paper, 8 1/2" x 11"
  pencils, colored, 16 or more

Keywords and Pronunciation

Palestine (PA-luh-stiyn)
Seljuk (sel-JOOK)

LEARN
Activity 1: Reviewing Feudalism *(Online)*

Activity 2: A New Bakery in Town *(Online)*

Activity 3: Show You Know *(Online)*

Activity 4: History Record Book *(Online)*

Activity 5. Optional: Growing Towns *(Online)*

Activity 6. Optional: Apprenticeships *(Online)*

ASSESS

Lesson Assessment: Towns and Trade *(Online)*

You will complete an offline assessment covering the main objectives of this lesson. Your learning coach will score this assessment.

LEARN

Activity 7. Optional: Explore Life in a Medieval Town *(Online)*

Activity 6. Optional: Apprenticeships *(Online)*

Name

Date

Growing Towns

What were medieval towns like? Circle the phrases on the right that describe medieval towns, then color the scene below.

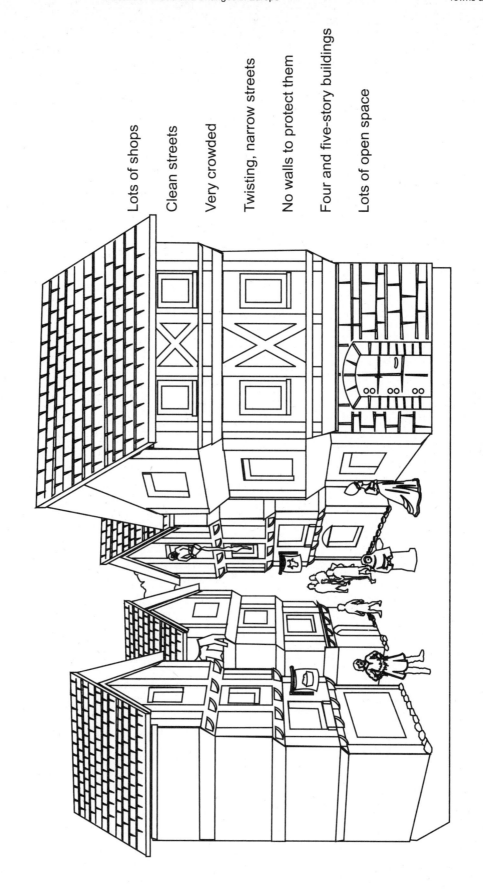

Lots of shops

Clean streets

Very crowded

Twisting, narrow streets

No walls to protect them

Four and five-story buildings

Lots of open space

Lesson Assessment

Towns and Trade

1. Why did medieval towns grow?

2. How would you describe medieval towns? Give two or more characteristics.

3. What did medieval towns become centers of?

Student Guide
Lesson 8: The Black Death

Lesson Objectives

- Demonstrate mastery of important knowledge and skills in this unit.
- Define plague as a disease that strikes many people at once.
- Name Black Death as the plague that killed many people during the Middle Ages.
- Explain that the Crusades were wars between European Christians and Muslims for possession of Palestine and especially for the city of Jerusalem.
- Identify Jerusalem as being sacred to Jews, Christians, and Muslims.
- Name King Richard I of England as the "lion-hearted" warrior king.
- Name Robin Hood as the legendary English outlaw who stole from the rich and gave to the poor.
- Identify King John as a king of England.
- Identify 1215 as the year the Magna Carta was signed.
- Name England and France as the two countries that fought the Hundred Years' War.
- Explain that Joan of Arc said she had visions telling her to lead the French army.
- Describe two characteristics of medieval towns, such as they had lots of shops and narrow twisting streets.

PREPARE

Approximate lesson time is 60 minutes.

Materials

For the Student
Optional
    🖳 The Plague Spreads activity sheet
    Elmer's Glue-All
    pencils, colored, 16 or more
    scissors, round-end safety

LEARN
Activity 1: Review *(Online)*

Activity 2: The Black Death Strikes Europe *(Online)*

Activity 3. Optional: The Plague Spreads *(Online)*

Activity 4: Unit Review *(Online)*

ASSESS

Unit Assessment: Crusades Abroad &Changes in Europe (*Offline*)

Complete an offline Unit Assessment. Your learning coach will score this part of the Assessment.

The Plague Spreads

Color the drawings at the bottom, then cut them out. Glue them in the correct squares to show how the plague spread.

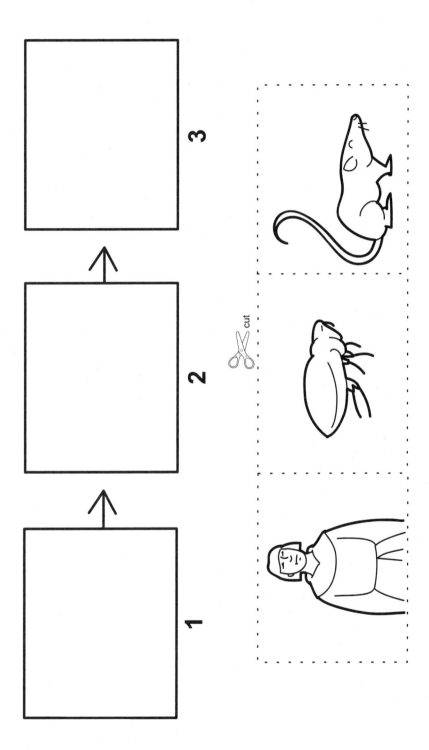

Name _____ Date _____

Crusades Abroad and Changes in Europe

Read each sentence and its answer choices. Fill in the bubble in front of the word or words that best answer the question.

1. What were the Crusades?
   - ○ wars between the English and the French for possession of France
   - ○ wars between Muslims and European Christians for possession of Palestine
   - ○ wars between King John and his nobles for possession of England

2. Which two countries fought each other in the Hundred Years' War?
   - ○ England and Spain
   - ○ Italy and France
   - ○ England and France

3. In what year was the Magna Carta signed?
   - ○ 1215
   - ○ 1492
   - ○ 1776

4. Which of the following choices correctly describes medieval towns?
   - ○ They were surrounded by walls and were very clean.
   - ○ They were very dirty and had twisting, narrow streets.
   - ○ They had wide, straight streets and had lots of shops.

5. What city is sacred to Jews, Muslims, and Christians?
   - ○ Constantinople
   - ○ Paris
   - ○ Jerusalem

6. What was the name of the plague that killed many people during the Middle Ages?
   ○ the Rat Plague
   ○ the Black Death
   ○ the Dark Boils Sickness

7. Who had visions and led the French against the English during the Hundred Years' War?
   ○ Saladin
   ○ Prince Charles
   ○ Joan of Arc

8. What English king became known as the "Lion-Heart" and fought in the Crusades?
   ○ Richard
   ○ John
   ○ Charlemagne

9. Who lived in Sherwood Forest and stole from the rich to give to the poor?
   ○ Joan of Arc
   ○ Robin Hood
   ○ King John

10. Who was forced to sign the Magna Carta?
    ○ King John
    ○ King Richard
    ○ Prince Charles

Student Guide
Lesson 1: Welcome to Africa!

Travel to Africa to see endless deserts, medieval kingdoms, and fabled trade routes. Meet the Mali hero Sundiata, King Mansa Musa, explorer Ibn Battuta, and Ethiopian King Lalibela. Explore Ghana and Mali, where salt was worth as much as gold. Journey along the Niger River and visit Timbuktu.

Lesson Objectives
- Locate Africa on a globe.
- Locate the Nile, Niger, and Congo Rivers on a map of Africa.
- Identify, locate, and describe the Sahara desert.
- Describe the savanna as grassland.

PREPARE

Approximate lesson time is 60 minutes.

Materials
For the Student
- map of Medieval Africa

Optional
- Regions of Africa activity sheet
- globe, inflatable
- crayons, 16 or more
- pencils, colored, 16 or more
- pencils, no. 2
- paper, 8 1/2" x 11"
- cardboard, sheets
- clay, colored
- grass clippings
- sand
- Elmer's Glue-All

Keywords and Pronunciation
Niger (NIY-jur)
oasis (oh-AY-sis) : A green or fertile area in a desert.
Sahara (suh-HAIR-uh)
savanna : A grassland containing a few scattered trees and some undergrowth.

LEARN
Activity 1: A Review of the Continents *(Online)*

Activity 2: Beginning a Study of Africa *(Online)*

Activity 3: The Continent of Africa *(Online)*

Activity 4: Show You Know *(Online)*

Activity 5: History Record Book *(Online)*

Activity 6. Optional: Making a Map of Africa *(Online)*

ASSESS

Lesson Assessment: Welcome to Africa! (*Online*)
You will complete an offline assessment covering the main objectives of this lesson. Your learning coach will score this assessment.

LEARN
Activity 7. Optional: Regions of Africa *(Online)*

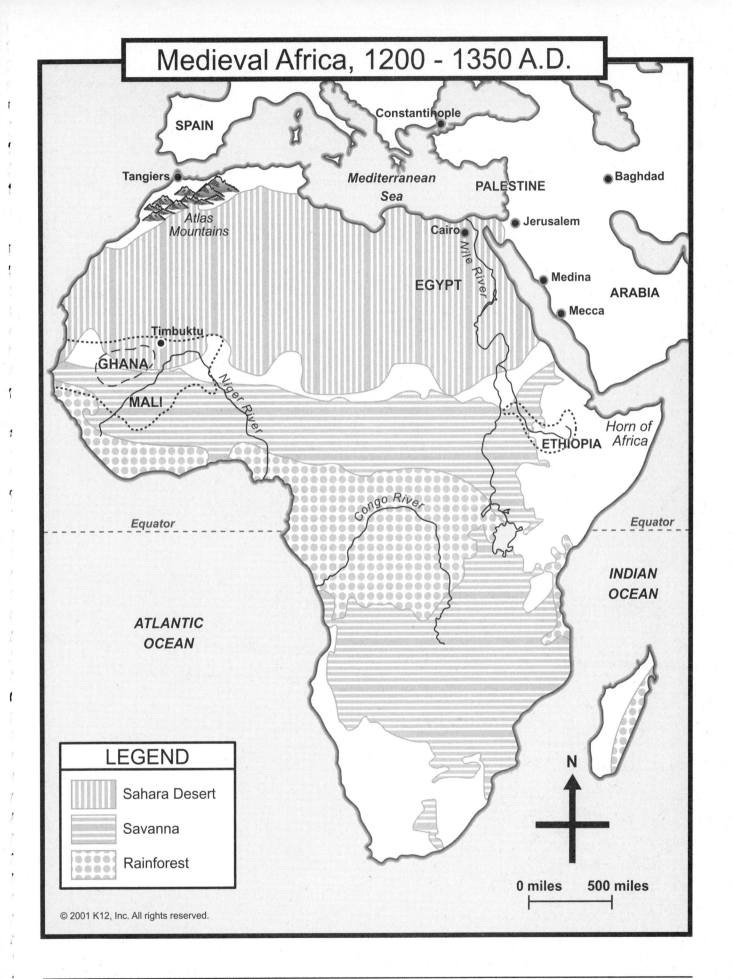

Medieval Africa, 1200 - 1350 A.D.

SPAIN

Constantinople

Mediterranean
Sea

PALESTINE

Baghdad

Tangiers

Atlas
Mountains

Cairo

Jerusalem

EGYPT

Nile River

Medina

ARABIA

Mecca

Timbuktu

GHANA

MALI

Niger River

Horn of
Africa

ETHIOPIA

Equator

Equator

Congo River

INDIAN
OCEAN

ATLANTIC
OCEAN

N

LEGEND

Sahara Desert

Savanna

Rainforest

0 miles   500 miles

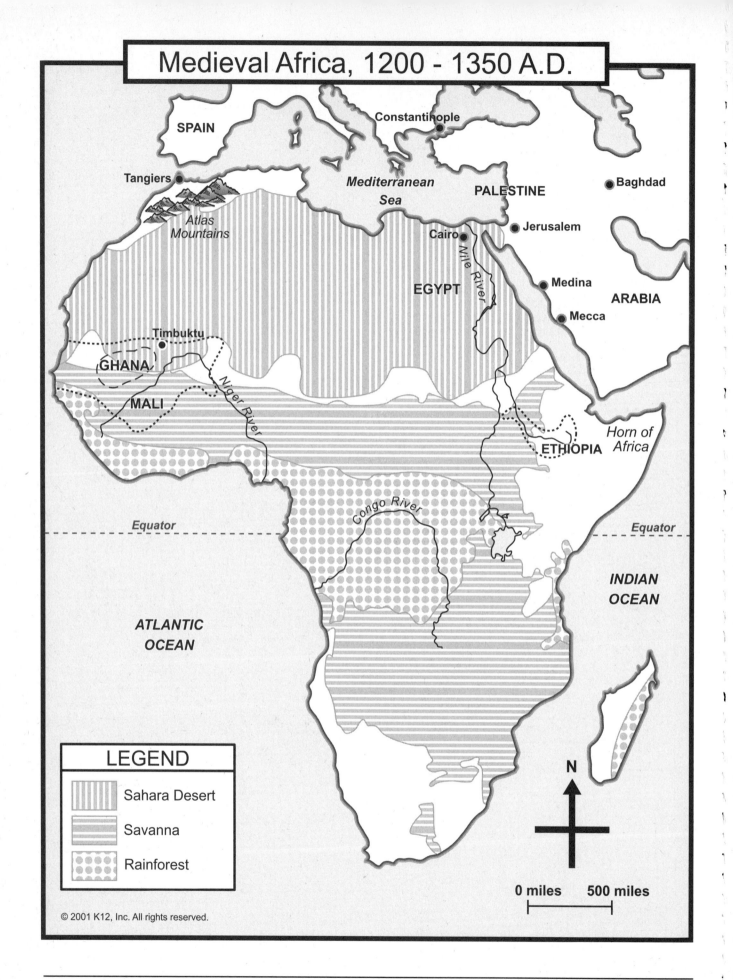

Medieval Africa, 1200 - 1350 A.D.

SPAIN

Constantinople

Tangiers

Mediterranean Sea

PALESTINE

Baghdad

Atlas Mountains

Cairo

Jerusalem

EGYPT

Nile River

Medina

ARABIA

Mecca

Timbuktu

GHANA

MALI

Niger River

Horn of Africa

ETHIOPIA

Congo River

Equator

Equator

INDIAN OCEAN

ATLANTIC OCEAN

N

LEGEND

Sahara Desert

Savanna

Rainforest

0 miles   500 miles

Name _____   Date _____

Regions of Africa

What region do you see in each picture? Use the words below to help you decide. Then label and color each picture.

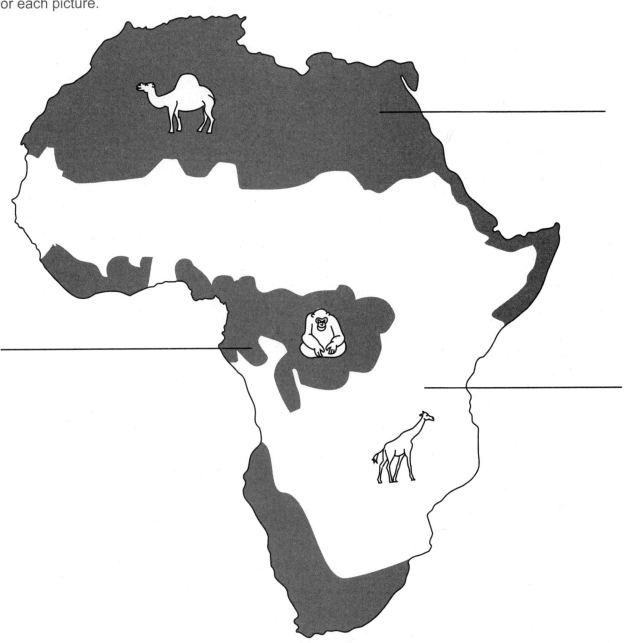

Word Bank

Sahara   rain forest   savanna

Lesson Assessment

Welcome to Africa!

1. Where is the Sahara on your map?

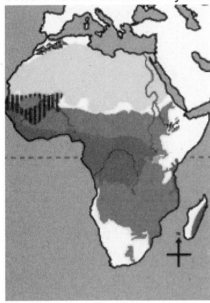

2. What words would you use to describe this desert?

3. We learned that south of the Sahara lies the savanna. What words would you use to describe the savanna?

4. The map of Africa shows three rivers. Which one is the Nile River? The Niger? The Congo?

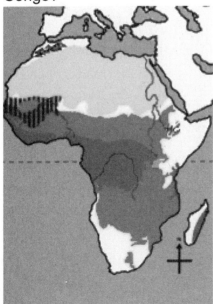

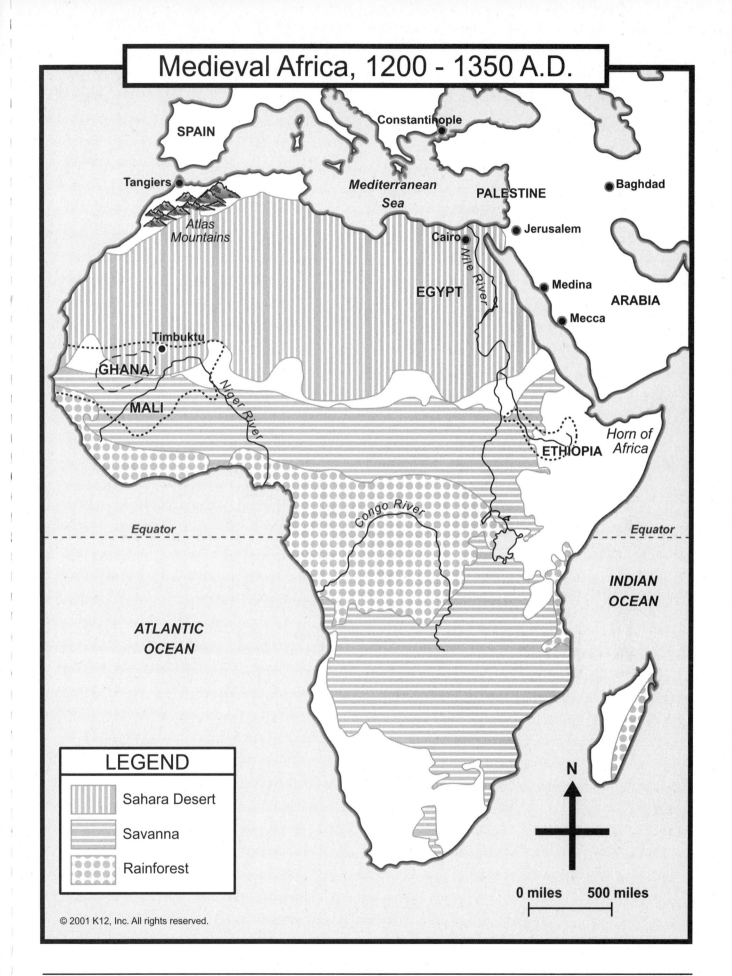

Medieval Africa, 1200 - 1350 A.D.

SPAIN

Constantinople

Mediterranean Sea

PALESTINE

Baghdad

Tangiers

Atlas Mountains

Cairo

Jerusalem

Nile River

EGYPT

Medina

ARABIA

Mecca

Timbuktu

GHANA

Niger River

MALI

ETHIOPIA

Horn of Africa

Congo River

Equator

Equator

INDIAN OCEAN

ATLANTIC OCEAN

LEGEND

Sahara Desert

Savanna

Rainforest

N

0 miles   500 miles

Student Guide
Lesson 2: Ghana: A Gold Kingdom

Lesson Objectives

- Demonstrate mastery of important knowledge and skills taught in previous lessons.
- Identify Ghana as a great kingdom in western Africa.
- Explain that merchants from Ghana traded gold for salt.
- Describe how traders used camels to cross the Sahara.

PREPARE

Approximate lesson time is 60 minutes.

Materials

For the Student

   📖 map of Medieval Africa

Optional

   📖 Camels Cross the Desert activity sheet

   📖 Gold and Salt in Ghana activity sheet

    map, world

    pencils, no. 2

    paper, 8 1/2" x 11"

    pencils, colored, 16 or more

    crayons, 16 or more

    salt

    Elmer's Glue-All

    glitter - gold

    paper, colored construction, 12"x12" - brown - small pieces

    egg carton, foam - 1 white, 1 yellow

    markers, colored, 8 or more

    pipe cleaners

    scissors, adult

    scissors, round-end safety

    Just So Stories by Rudyard Kipling

Keywords and Pronunciation

Ghana (GAH-nuh)

LEARN
Activity 1: Review of African Geography *(Online)*

Activity 2: Salt for Gold *(Online)*

Activity 3: Show You Know *(Online)*

Activity 4: History Record Book *(Online)*

Activity 5. Optional: Gold and Salt in Ghana *(Online)*

Activity 6. Optional: Camels Cross the Desert *(Online)*

ASSESS
Lesson Assessment: Ghana: A Gold Kingdom (*Online*)

You will complete an offline assessment covering the main objectives of this lesson. Your learning coach will score this assessment.

LEARN
Activity 7. Optional: How the Camel Got His Hump *(Online)*

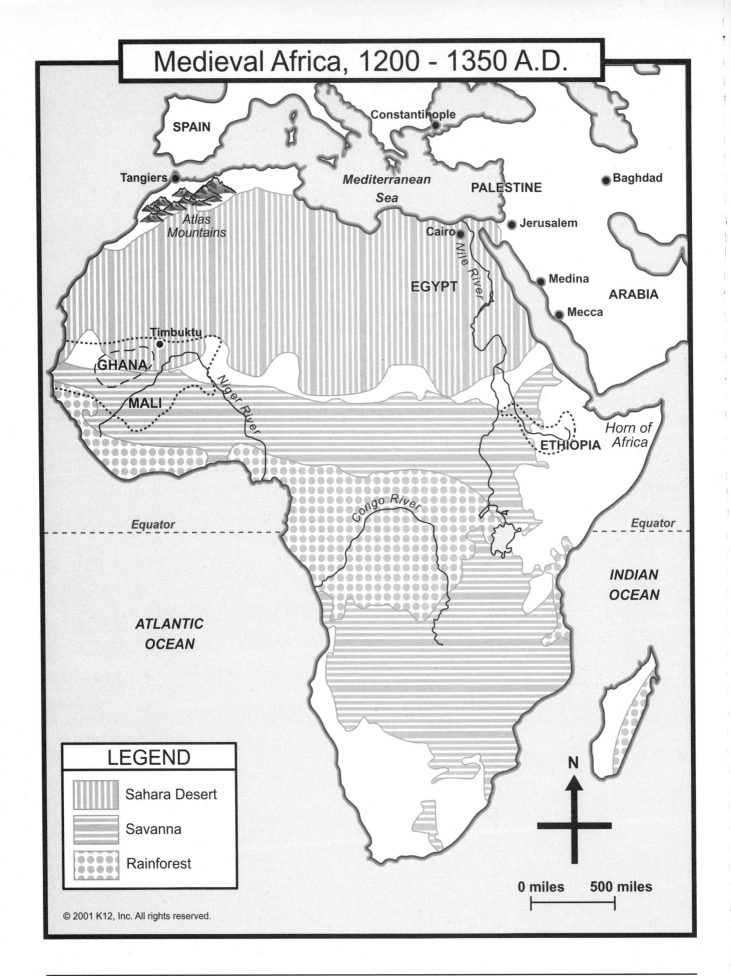

Medieval Africa, 1200 - 1350 A.D.

SPAIN

Tangiers

Atlas Mountains

Mediterranean Sea

Constantinople

PALESTINE

Baghdad

Cairo

Jerusalem

Medina

Mecca

ARABIA

EGYPT

Nile River

Timbuktu

GHANA

MALI

Niger River

ETHIOPIA

Horn of Africa

Congo River

Equator

Equator

INDIAN OCEAN

ATLANTIC OCEAN

N

LEGEND

Sahara Desert

Savanna

Rainforest

0 miles   500 miles

Camels Cross the Desert

Follow the steps below to make two camels. One is for the spices and silk Ali brought to trade. The other is for the gold that Tunka brought to trade.

Take one eggcup from a yellow Styrofoam egg carton, and one from a white Styrofoam egg carton.

1. Ask an adult to use the point of a scissors to help you. The adult should make 4 holes at the bottom of each eggcup. These are for the legs.

2. Then the adult should make holes at the ends of each eggcup. These are for the camels' necks and tails.

3. Draw heads for your camels on a piece of brown construction paper. You will need to draw a total of four head shapes.

4. Lay a pipe cleaner between two of the head shapes. Then glue them together with the pipe cleaner in between to make the head for one camel. Make two heads.

5. Attach one head to each egg carton.

6. Use four pipe cleaners to add legs and feet to each camel.

7. Use two more pipe cleaners to add tails.

8. Make eyes and mouths for your camels with your markers.

Now use your camels to tell a story about their travels with Ali and Tunka.

Name _____   Date _____

Gold and Salt

Cover each thing in Ali's thoughts with a little bit of glue. Then put gold glitter on top of it. Cover each thing in Tunka's thoughts with glue and put salt on top of that. Then color the picture.

Name _____ Date _____

Lesson Assessment

Ghana: A Gold Kingdom

1. In what part of Africa was the kingdom of Ghana located?

2. What was the kingdom of Ghana famous for?

3. What did the merchants of Ghana often trade their gold for?

4. What animal helped traders cross the Sahara?

Student Guide
Lesson 3: Sundiata: Lion King of Mali

Lesson Objectives
- Demonstrate mastery of important knowledge and skills taught in previous lessons.
- Identify Mali as an African kingdom.
- Explain the problems that Sundiata overcame to become king of Mali.

PREPARE

Approximate lesson time is 60 minutes.

Materials

For the Student
- 📖 *Sundiata: Lion King of Mali* questions
- 📖 map of Medieval Africa

Optional
- 📖 Sundiata Rules an African Kingdom activity sheet
- 📖 Sundiata: Lion King of Mali activity sheet
- 📖 Sundiata: Lion King of Mali questions

  Sundiata: Lion King of Mali written and illustrated by David Wisniewski (ISBN 0-395-76481-5)

  pencils, no. 2

  paper, 8 1/2" x 11"

  pencils, colored, 16 or more

  paper, colored construction, 12"x12" - variety of colors

  Elmer's Glue-All

  scissors, round-end safety

  crayons, 16 or more

  musical instruments

Keywords and Pronunciation
griots (GREE-ohz)

Mali (MAH-lee)

Sumanguru (soo-mahng-GOO-roo)

Sundiata (soun-JAH-tah)

LEARN
Activity 1: Review *(Online)*

Activity 2: Sundiata's Story (Online)

Activity 3: Show You Know (Online)

Activity 4: History Record Book (Online)

Activity 5. Optional: Sundiata Illustration (Online)

Activity 6. Optional: Sundiata Rules an African Kingdom (Online)

ASSESS

Lesson Assessment: Sundiata: Lion King of Mali (*Online*)

You will complete an offline assessment covering the main objectives of this lesson. Your learning coach will score this assessment.

LEARN

Activity 7. Optional: Sing a Song of Sundiata (Online)

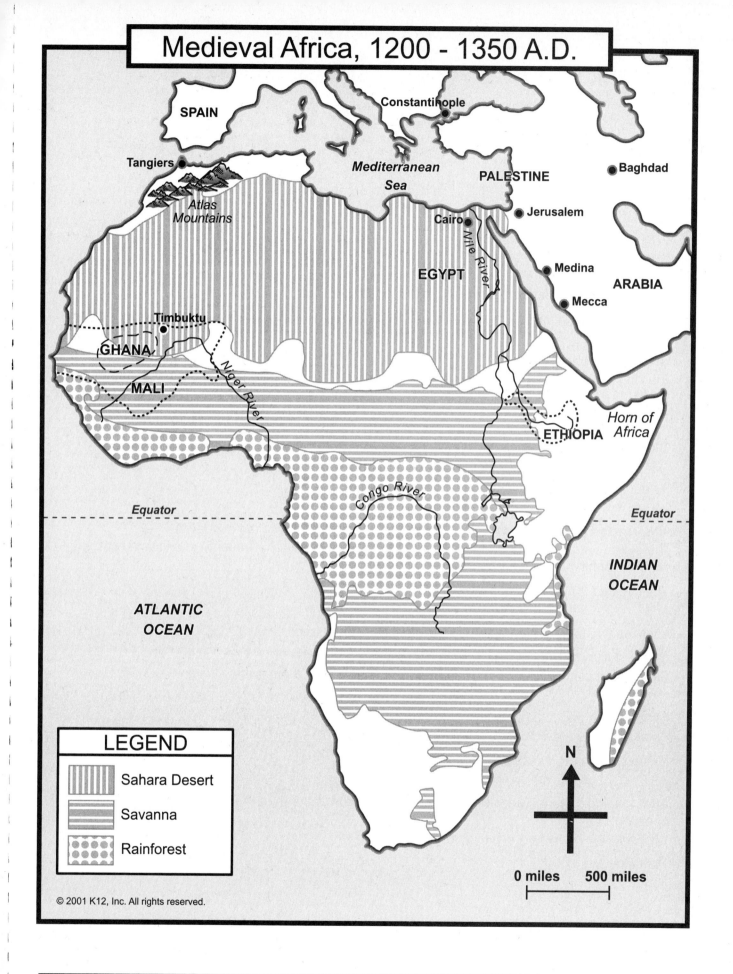

Medieval Africa, 1200 - 1350 A.D.

SPAIN

Constantinople

Mediterranean Sea

PALESTINE

• Baghdad

Tangiers •

Atlas Mountains

Cairo •

Jerusalem •

EGYPT

Nile River

• Medina

ARABIA

• Mecca

• Timbuktu

GHANA

MALI

Niger River

ETHIOPIA

Horn of Africa

Congo River

Equator

Equator

INDIAN OCEAN

ATLANTIC OCEAN

LEGEND

|||| Sahara Desert

─── Savanna

••• Rainforest

N

0 miles   500 miles

© 2001 K12, Inc. All rights reserved.

Sundiata: Lion King of Mali Discussion Questions

The pages of *Sundiata: Lion King of Mali* are not numbered. For the purposes of the suggested discussion questions, page 1 is the first page of the story. It begins, "Listen to me, children of the Bright Country, and hear the great deeds of ages past." As always, it is important to preview the book before you read it aloud.

After reading page 2 (ends with ". . . to walk with greatness"), ask the question:
Who is telling this story?

a griot

After reading page 6 (ends with "At this, Sassouma Berete rejoiced"), ask the question:
How was Sundiata different from the other children?

He couldn't walk or talk.

After reading page 10 (ends with ". . . and he prepared Sundiata to rule"), ask the question:
The king is going to make Sundiata the next king. How do you think Sundiata's stepmother will feel?

angry, jealous

After reading page 11 (ends with "The lion is walking!"), ask the question:
How did Sundiata start walking?

He put a rod in the ground and pulled himself up.

After reading page 16 (ends with ". . . they knew and loved"), ask the question:
The queen tried to use magic against Sundiata. Then she sent his best friend, his griot, away to another country. What did Sundiata's mother decide they must do?

She decided they must leave Mali.

After reading page 20 (ends with "Your destiny is about to be fulfilled"), ask the question:
Why do the people of Mali want Sundiata to come back?

Sumunguru has invaded Mali. They want Sundiata to help them and be king.

After reading page 25 (ends with ". . . the sorcerer's army went down to defeat"), ask the question:
What happened to Sumanguru (soo-mahng-GOO-roo)?

He fled to a cave; it is said he turned into stone in the cave.

After reading page 28 (ends with ". . . ruled the Bright Country for many golden years"), ask the question:
Who won the battle for the kingdom of Mali?

Sundiata

Sundiata Rules an African Kingdom

Draw the border around the ancient kingdom of Mali. Lightly color or shade in the area inside this kingdom. Then draw a picture of Sundiata inside of Africa watching over his kingdom.

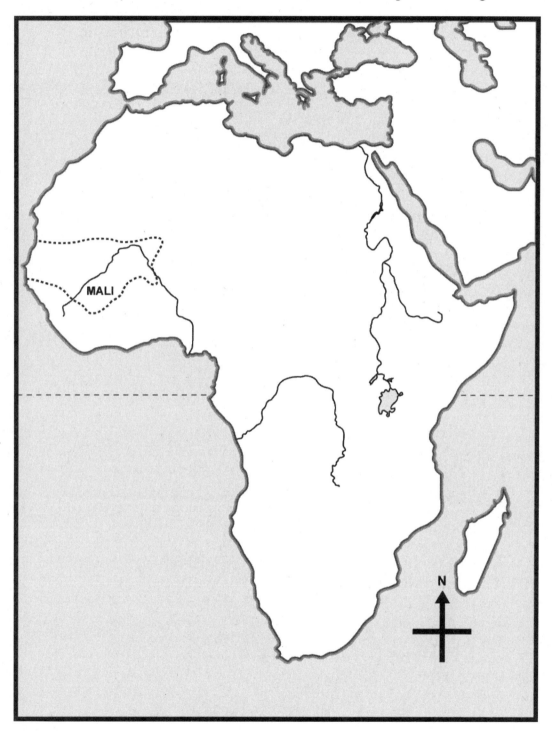

Name _____   Date _____

Sundiata: Lion King of Mali

Cut out small pieces of construction paper, and glue them on this picture to make your lion king look fierce and brave. In the caption at the bottom, write his name and the name of his country.

_____ : Lion King of _____

Lesson Assessment

Sundiata: Lion King of Mali

1. What was the name of the kingdom we read about today?

2. Where was this kingdom located?

3. What problems did Sundiata have as a child?

Student Guide
Lesson 4: Mansa Musa of Mali

Lesson Objectives
- Demonstrate mastery of important knowledge and skills taught in previous lessons.
- Identify Mansa Musa as a wealthy ruler of Mali.
- Explain that Mansa Musa made a famous pilgrimage to Mecca.
- Identify Mali as an African kingdom.

PREPARE

Approximate lesson time is 60 minutes.

Materials

For the Student

    📖 map of Medieval Africa

Optional

    📖 Mansa Musa Gives Away Gold activity sheet

    📖 Traveling with Mansa Musa activity sheet

    pencils, no. 2

    paper, 8 1/2" x 11"

    pencils, colored, 16 or more

    crayons, 16 or more

    globe, inflatable

Keywords and Pronunciation

Cairo (KIY-roh)

Mansa (MAHN-sah)

Mansa Musa (MAHN-sah moo-SAH)

Sumanguru (soo-mahng-GOO-roo)

LEARN
Activity 1: Ghana and Mali Review *(Online)*

Activity 2: Mansa Musa's Long Journey *(Online)*

Activity 3: Show You Know *(Online)*

Activity 4: History Record Book *(Online)*

Activity 5. Optional: Mansa Musa Gives Away Gold *(Online)*

Activity 6. Optional: Traveling with Mansa Musa *(Online)*

ASSESS
Lesson Assessment: Mansa Musa of Mali (*Online*)
You will complete an offline assessment covering the main objectives of this lesson. Your learning coach will score this assessment.

LEARN
Activity 7. Optional: Mali Then and Now *(Online)*

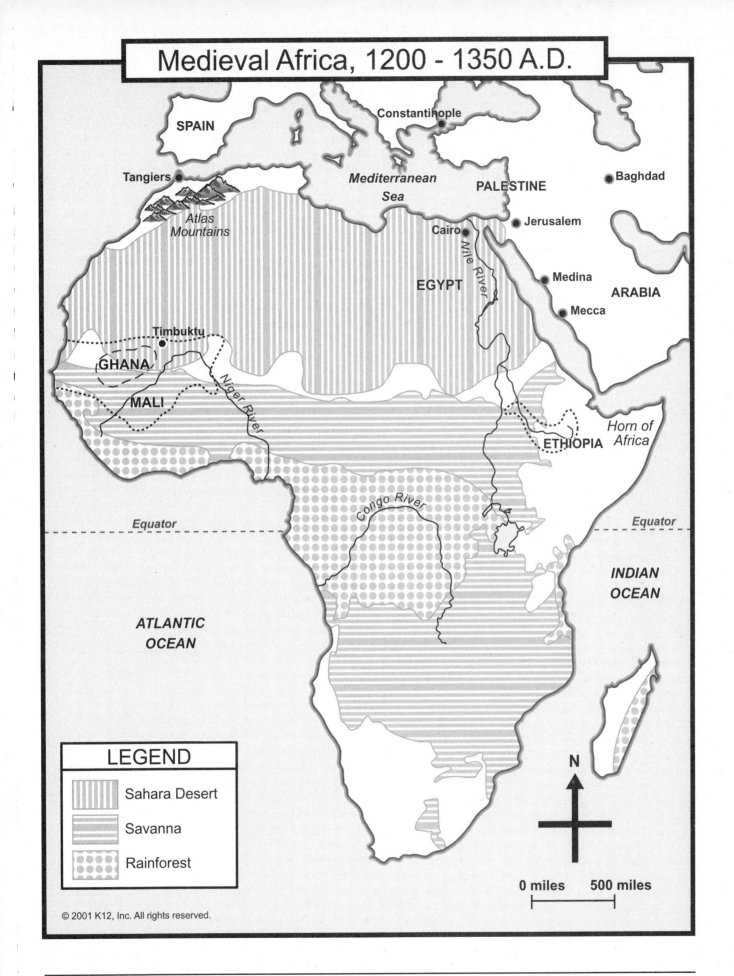

Medieval Africa, 1200 - 1350 A.D.

SPAIN

Constantinople

Mediterranean Sea

PALESTINE

Baghdad

Tangiers

Atlas Mountains

Cairo

Jerusalem

Nile River

EGYPT

Medina

ARABIA

Mecca

Timbuktu

GHANA

MALI

Niger River

Horn of Africa

ETHIOPIA

Equator

Congo River

Equator

INDIAN OCEAN

ATLANTIC OCEAN

N

LEGEND

Sahara Desert

Savanna

Rainforest

0 miles   500 miles

Traveling with Mansa Musa

Mansa Musa Gives Away Gold

Show Mansa Musa's travels. Choose a color to fill in the dot next to Mecca. Use the same color to mark Mecca in the key. Choose another color, and do the same for Cairo. Then color the area showing Mali on the map and in the key. Trace over the outline of the continent of Africa with another color. Finally, color the picture of Mansa Musa giving away gold.

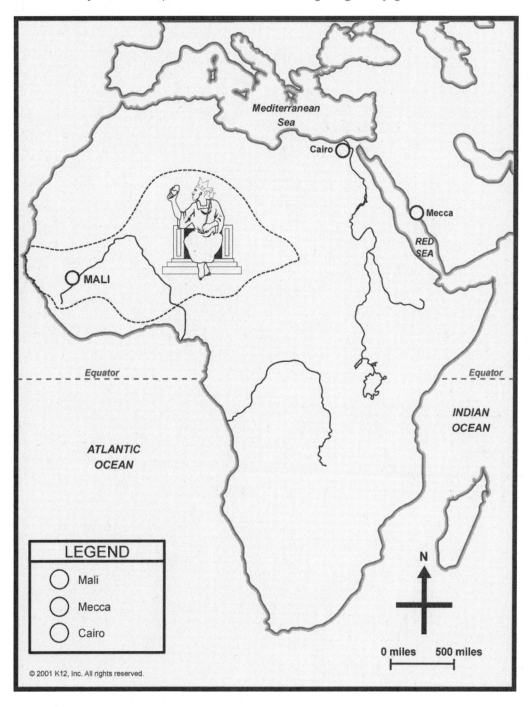

Lesson Assessment

Mansa Musa of Mali

1. What was Sundiata's grandson's name?

2. Was Mansa Musa a poor king, or did he have many riches?

3. Mansa Musa made a famous religious journey. Where did he go?

Student Guide
Lesson 5: All the Way to Timbuktu

Lesson Objectives
- Demonstrate mastery of important knowledge and skills taug
- Locate Timbuktu on a map.
- Show that Timbuktu was near the Niger River.
- Identify Timbuktu as a center of trade and learning.

PREPARE

Approximate lesson time is 60 minutes.

Materials

For the Student

    🖳 map of Medieval Africa

    🖳 Where Is Timbuktu? activity sheet

    pencils, no. 2

    paper, 8 1/2" x 11"

    pencils, colored, 16 or more

Optional

    clay, colored

    sand

    water

    Koi and the Kola Nuts by Verna Aardema

Keywords and Pronunciation

kola (KOH-luh)

Timbuktu (tim-buhk-TOO)

LEARN
Activity 1: Review of Mansa Musa's Pilgrimage (O

Activity 2: Timbuktu: A Center of Learning (Online)

Activity 3: Show You Know (Online)

Activity 4: History Record

Activity 5. Optional: Buildi *(Online)*

Activity 6. Optional: Wher *(Online)*

ASSESS

Lesson Assessment: All **uktu** (*Online*)

You will complete an offline assess¹ objectives of this lesson. Your learning coach will score this assessment.

LEARN

Activity 7. Optional: *Koi ₴* (*Online*)

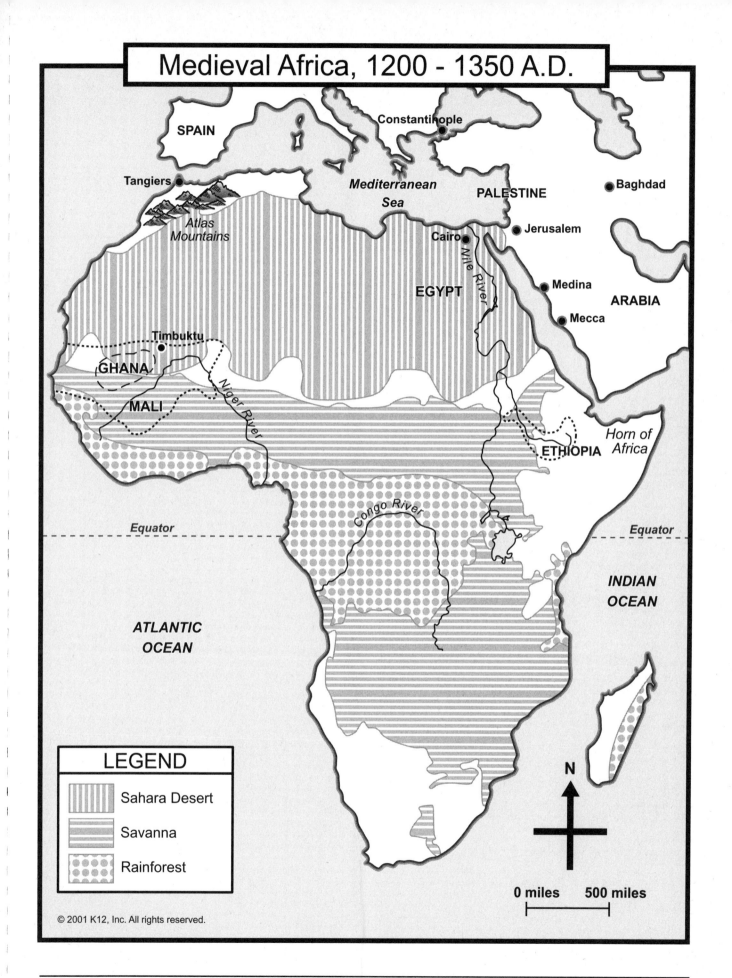

Medieval Africa, 1200 - 1350 A.D.

SPAIN

Constantinople

Mediterranean Sea

PALESTINE

Baghdad

Tangiers

Atlas Mountains

Cairo

Jerusalem

Nile River

EGYPT

Medina

ARABIA

Mecca

Timbuktu

GHANA

MALI

Niger River

ETHIOPIA

Horn of Africa

Congo River

Equator

Equator

INDIAN OCEAN

ATLANTIC OCEAN

LEGEND

	Sahara Desert
	Savanna
	Rainforest

N

0 miles   500 miles

Name _____   Date _____

Where is Timbuktu?

Use the words in the word box to fill in the blanks and label the places. Then mark the line of the river blue to show the flow of the water. Outline the country in a different color. Use the same color to show its location on the picture of the globe.

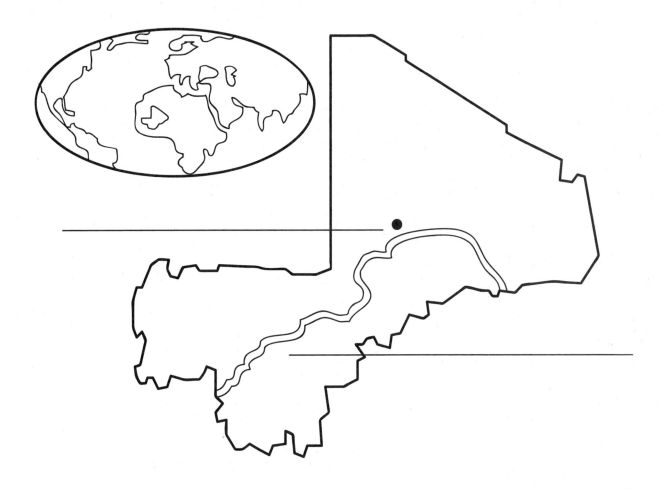

This is the ancient kingdom of _____.

It is on the continent of _____.

Word Bank

Africa	Mali	Niger	Timbuktu

Name _____   Date _____

Lesson Assessment

All the Way to Timbuktu

1. Locate Timbuktu on your map.

2. What river is Timbuktu near?

3. People took them there for trade.

4. Timbuktu was a great center of learning.

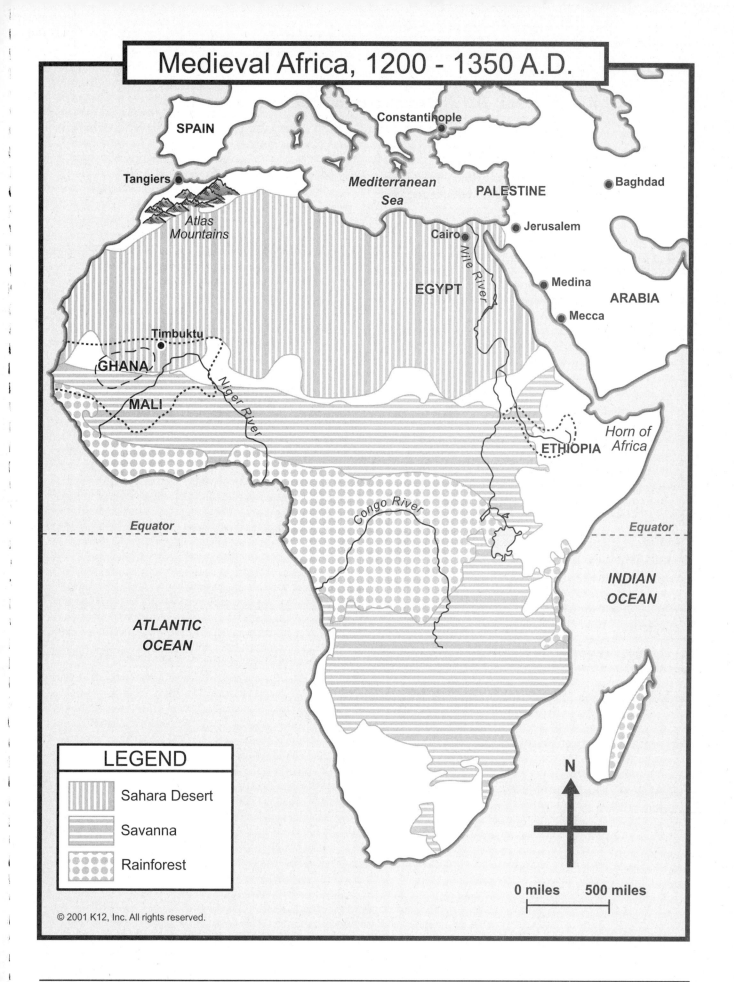

Medieval Africa, 1200 - 1350 A.D.

SPAIN

Constantinople

Tangiers

Mediterranean Sea

PALESTINE

Baghdad

Atlas Mountains

Cairo

Jerusalem

EGYPT

Nile River

Medina

Mecca

ARABIA

Timbuktu

GHANA

MALI

Niger River

ETHIOPIA

Horn of Africa

Congo River

Equator

Equator

INDIAN OCEAN

ATLANTIC OCEAN

LEGEND

	Sahara Desert
	Savanna
	Rainforest

N

0 miles   500 miles

245

Student Guide
Lesson 6: Ibn Battuta: An Amazing Traveler

Lesson Objectives
- Demonstrate mastery of important knowledge and skills taught in previous lessons.
- Identify Ibn Battuta as a famous Muslim explorer.
- Explain that Ibn Battuta traveled in Africa, Europe, and Asia.

PREPARE

Approximate lesson time is 60 minutes.

Materials
For the Student
    🖥 map of Medieval Africa
    pencils, no. 2
    paper, 8 1/2" x 11"
    pencils, colored, 16 or more
Optional
    crayons, 16 or more
    paper, drawing, 12" x 18"
    Traveling Man: The Journey of Ibn Battuta by James Rumford

Keywords and Pronunciation
Ibn Battuta (IB-uhn bat-TOO-tah)
Tangiers (tan-JIHRZ)

LEARN
Activity 1: Reviewing Mansa Musa *(Online)*

Activity 2: The Many Journeys of Ibn Battuta *(Online)*

Activity 3: Show You Know *(Online)*

Activity 4: History Record Book *(Online)*

Activity 5. Optional: Ibn Battuta: By the Numbers *(Online)*

Activity 6. Optional: If Ibn Battuta Had a Camera *(Online)*

ASSESS

Lesson Assessment: Ibn Battuta: An Amazing Traveler *(Online)*

You will complete an offline assessment covering the main objectives of this lesson. Your learning coach will score this assessment.

LEARN

Activity 7. Optional: Where Is Ibn Battuta? *(Online)*

Activity 8. Optional: Ibn Battuta: The Traveling Man *(Online)*

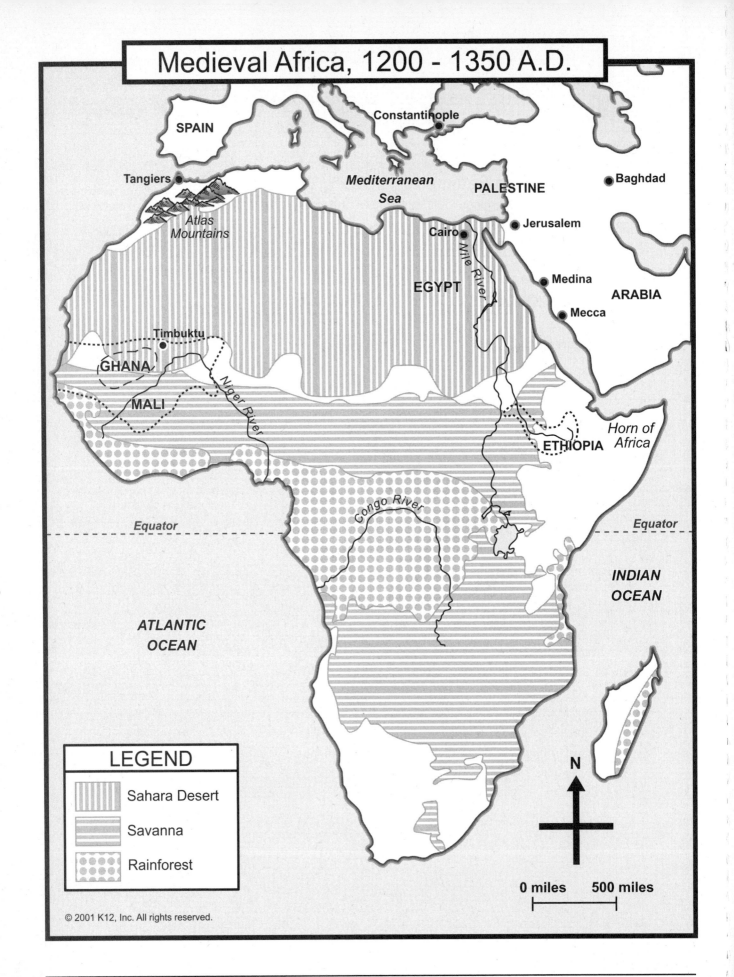

Medieval Africa, 1200 - 1350 A.D.

SPAIN

Tangiers

Atlas Mountains

Mediterranean Sea

Constantinople

PALESTINE

Baghdad

Jerusalem

Cairo

Nile River

EGYPT

Medina

Mecca

ARABIA

Timbuktu

GHANA

MALI

Niger River

ETHIOPIA

Horn of Africa

Congo River

Equator

Equator

INDIAN OCEAN

ATLANTIC OCEAN

LEGEND

	Sahara Desert
	Savanna
	Rainforest

N

0 miles   500 miles

Lesson Assessment

Ibn Battuta: An Amazing Traveler

1. Why was Ibn Battuta famous?

2. What religion did Ibn Battuta follow?

3. What are some of the places where Ibn Battuta traveled?

Student Guide
Lesson 7: King Lalibela's Churches in Stone

Lesson Objectives
- Demonstrate mastery of important knowledge and skills taught in previous lessons.
- Demonstrate mastery of important knowledge and skills in this unit.
- Identify, locate, and describe the Sahara desert.
- Describe the savanna as grassland.
- Explain that merchants from Ghana traded gold for salt.
- Describe how traders used camels to cross the Sahara.
- Explain the problems that Sundiata overcame to become king of Mali.
- Explain that Mansa Musa made a famous pilgrimage to Mecca.
- Show that Timbuktu was near the Niger River.
- Identify Timbuktu as a center of trade and learning.
- Identify Ibn Battuta as a famous Muslim explorer.
- Explain that King Lalibela is said to have built several stone churches.

PREPARE

Approximate lesson time is 60 minutes.

Materials
> For the Student
>> 🖥 map of Medieval Africa
> Optional
>> map, world

Keywords and Pronunciation
Ethiopia (ee-thee-OH-pee-uh)
Lalibela (lah-lee-BEL-uh)

LEARN
Activity 1: Where in Africa *(Online)*

Activity 2: Unit Review *(Online)*

ASSESS

Unit Assessment: Medieval African Empires (*Offline*)
Complete an offline Unit Assessment. Your learning coach will score this part of the Assessment.

LEARN
Activity 3. Optional: The Mystery of Lalibela *(Online)*

Activity 4. Optional: Getting to Ethiopia *(Online)*

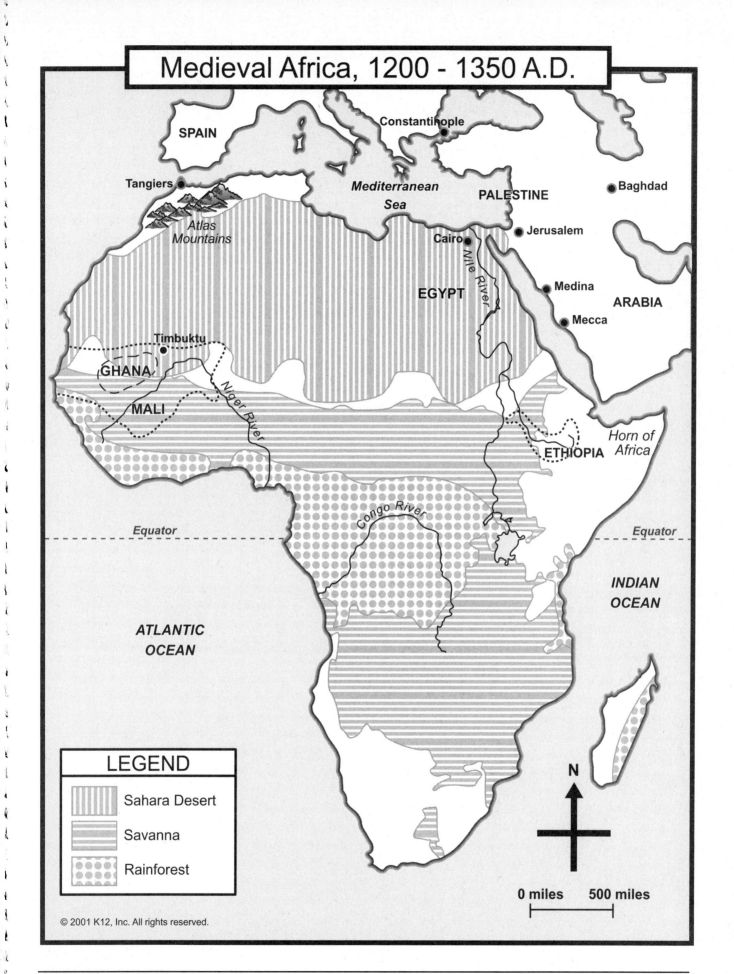

Medieval Africa, 1200 - 1350 A.D.

SPAIN

Constantinople

Mediterranean Sea

PALESTINE

Tangiers

Baghdad

Atlas Mountains

Cairo

Jerusalem

Nile River

EGYPT

Medina

ARABIA

Mecca

Timbuktu

GHANA

MALI

Niger River

Horn of Africa

ETHIOPIA

Congo River

Equator

Equator

INDIAN OCEAN

ATLANTIC OCEAN

LEGEND

Sahara Desert

Savanna

Rainforest

N

0 miles   500 miles

Name _____   Date _____

Medieval African Empires

Read each sentence and its answer choices. Fill in the bubble in front the word or words that best answer the question.

1. The Kingdoms of Ghana and Mali, and the city of Timbuktu grew up along the _____ River.
   - ○ Nile
   - ○ Niger
   - ○ Congo

2. In Ghana merchants traded
   - ○ cotton for jewels
   - ○ salt for furs
   - ○ gold for salt

3. Muslim merchants traveled across north Africa using
   - ○ camel caravans
   - ○ sailing ships
   - ○ covered wagons

4. Mansa Musa was known throughout Africa and Europe as a wealthy king who
   - ○ led his people to victory during the Crusades
   - ○ went on pilgrimage to Mecca and gave away gold
   - ○ started the kingdom of Mali by defeating Sumanguru

5. Sundiata was
- ○ known as Mali's founder and also as the "Lion King"
- ○ the explorer who discovered the Nile River
- ○ a person who founded a new religion

6. Ibn Battuta
- ○ wanted to travel but never crossed the Sahara
- ○ explored Africa and the world for more than 25 years
- ○ was the largest city in Ghana

7. The Sahara is a
- ○ desert
- ○ plain
- ○ hill

8. A city in Africa famous for its trade and learning was
- ○ Timbuktu
- ○ Mali
- ○ Ghana

9. The part of Africa called the savanna is
- ○ swamp
- ○ mountain
- ○ grassland

Student Guide
Lesson 1: Remembering Ancient China

Revisit ancient China, and then travel there during medieval times. Learn about ambitious dynasties. Sail the Grand Canal and walk along the Silk Road. Learn how Buddhism became important in China. Meet two outsiders--Genghis Khan and Marco Polo--as they visited China, one in war, one in peace.

Lesson Objectives
- Locate China on a map.
- Identify Confucius as a great Chinese teacher.
- State that the Chinese built the Great Wall as protection from invaders.
- Explain that silk production began in China.

PREPARE

Approximate lesson time is 60 minutes.

Materials

For the Student

     📖 map of Medieval China

Optional

     📖 Great Walls of China activity sheet

     📖 The Sayings of Confucius activity sheet

     crayons, 16 or more

     map, world

     pencils, no. 2

     paper, 8 1/2" x 11"

     pencils, colored, 16 or more

     clay, colored

     sand

     Elmer's Glue-All

     toothpicks

     The Empress and the Silkworm by Lily Toy Hong

Keywords and Pronunciation

Confucius (kuhn-FYOO-shuhs)

Han (hahn)

Qin Shi Huangdi (chin shur hwahng-dee)

Yangtze (YANG-see)

LEARN
Activity 1: Beginning an Asian Journey *(Online)*

Activity 2: Life in Ancient China *(Online)*

Activity 3: Confucius, the First Emperor, and a Great Wall *(Online)*

Activity 4: Show You Know *(Online)*

Activity 5: History Record Book *(Online)*

Activity 6. Optional: The Sayings of Confucius *(Online)*

Activity 7. Optional: Great Walls of China *(Online)*

ASSESS
Lesson Assessment: Remembering Ancient China (*Online*)
You will complete an offline assessment covering the main objectives of this lesson. Your learning coach will score this assessment.

LEARN
Activity 8. Optional: The Secret of Silk *(Online)*

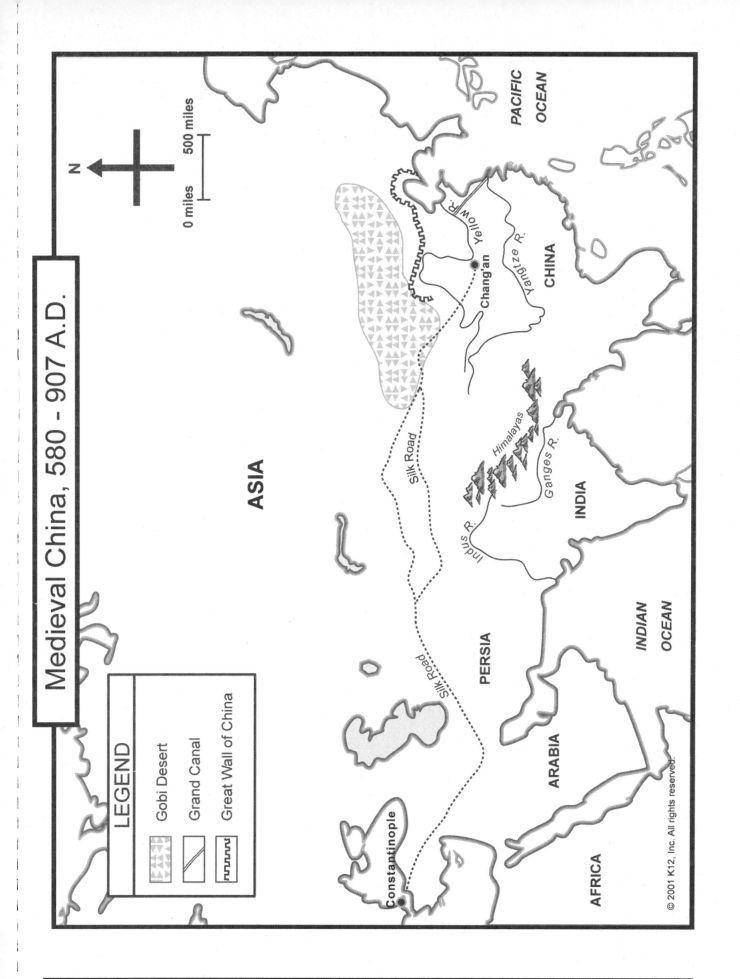

Medieval China, 580 – 907 A.D.

N

500 miles

0 miles

PACIFIC OCEAN

CHINA

Chang'an

Yellow R.

Yangtze R.

Himalayas

Ganges R.

Indus R.

INDIA

ASIA

Silk Road

PERSIA

INDIAN OCEAN

ARABIA

AFRICA

Constantinople

Silk Road

LEGEND

	Gobi Desert
	Grand Canal
	Great Wall of China

© 2001 K12, Inc. All rights reserved.

Name _____   Date _____

The Sayings of Confucius

Confucius was a great teacher. He loved learning and thinking. Here are some things he said. Choose one saying. Then draw a picture on the back to show what it means. Circle your choice first, and color the picture of Confucius, too.

It does not matter how slowly you go, so long as you do not stop.

No matter how much one knows, there is always more to learn.

Do not do to others what you would not like yourself.

Behave to everyone as if you were receiving a great guest.

I hear and I forget. I see and I remember. I do and I understand.

Name

Date

Great Walls of China

Follow the directions with each picture to make several Great Walls. Color the rest of each picture.
Put a star on the Great Wall you like best.

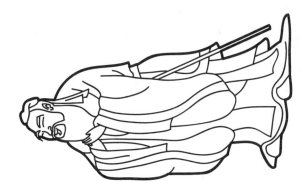

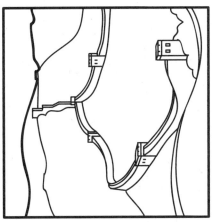

1. Put clay on this Great Wall to build it.

2. Color this Great Wall.

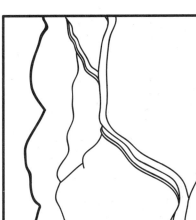

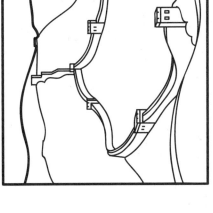

3. Cover this Great Wall with glue. Then add sand or dirt to build it.

4. Make this Great Wall and temple with glue and toothpicks.

Lesson Assessment

Remembering Ancient China

1. Locate China on the map.

2. What was the name of the new kind of cloth ancient Chinese people made?

3. What did the Chinese do to start making this new cloth?

4. What was the name of the great Chinese teacher who taught about respect and peaceful living?

5. What did the emperors of China build to guard against invaders from the north?

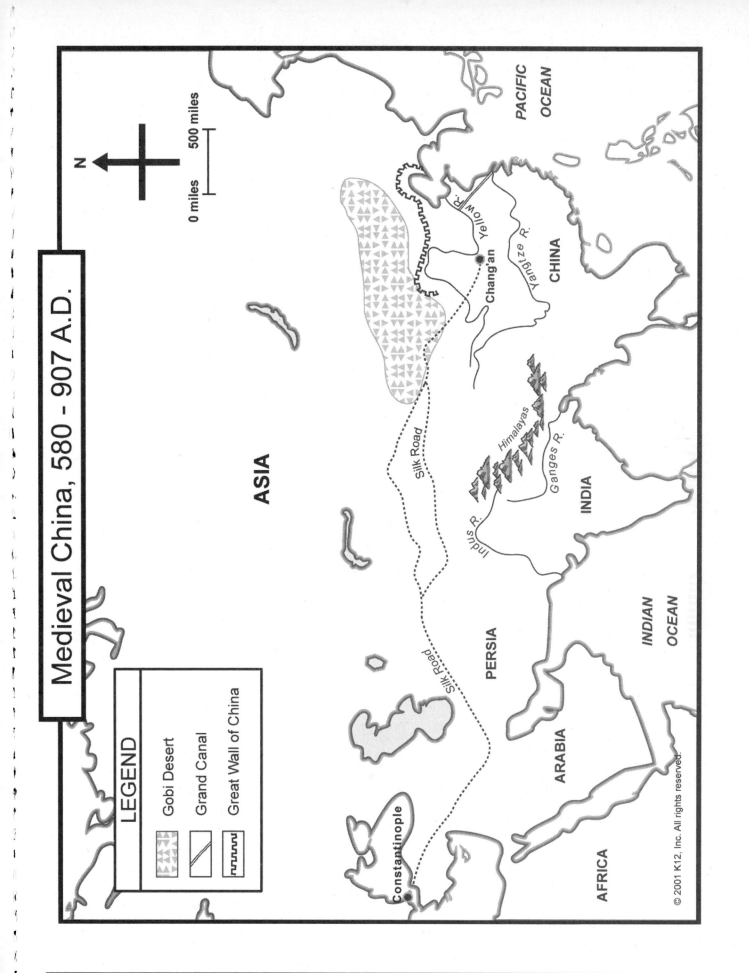

Medieval China, 580 – 907 A.D.

PACIFIC OCEAN

ASIA

CHINA

Chang'an

Yellow R.

Yangtze R.

Himalayas

Ganges R.

Indus R.

INDIA

Silk Road

PERSIA

Silk Road

Constantinople

ARABIA

AFRICA

INDIAN OCEAN

N

500 miles

0 miles

LEGEND

Gobi Desert

Grand Canal

Great Wall of China

© 2001 K12, Inc. All rights reserved.

Student Guide
Lesson 2: The Grand Canal

Lesson Objectives

- Locate the Yellow and Yangtze Rivers on map.
- Explain that the Grand Canal allowed the Chinese to ship rice and other goods between the north and the south.
- Identify the Grand Canal as a long, man-made waterway in China.
- Define a dynasty as a family that rules a country for many years.

PREPARE

Approximate lesson time is 60 minutes.

Materials

For the Student

  🖥 map of Medieval China

Optional

  🖥 Emperors Rule activity sheet

  🖥 Travel on the Grand Canal activity sheet

  pencils, no. 2

  paper, 8 1/2" x 11"

  pencils, colored, 16 or more

  paintbrush

  paints, watercolor, 8 colors or more

Keywords and Pronunciation

dynasty : A family that rules a country for many years.

Hua-Mei (hwah-may)

Sui (sway)

LEARN
Activity 1: Looking Back at Ancient China *(Online)*

Activity 2: Building the Grand Canal *(Online)*

Activity 3: Show You Know (*Online*)

Activity 4: History Record Book (*Online*)

Activity 5. Optional: Travel on the Grand Canal (*Online*)

Activity 6. Optional: Emperors Rule (*Online*)

ASSESS

Lesson Assessment: The Grand Canal (*Online*)

You will complete an offline assessment covering the main objectives of this lesson. Your learning coach will score this assessment.

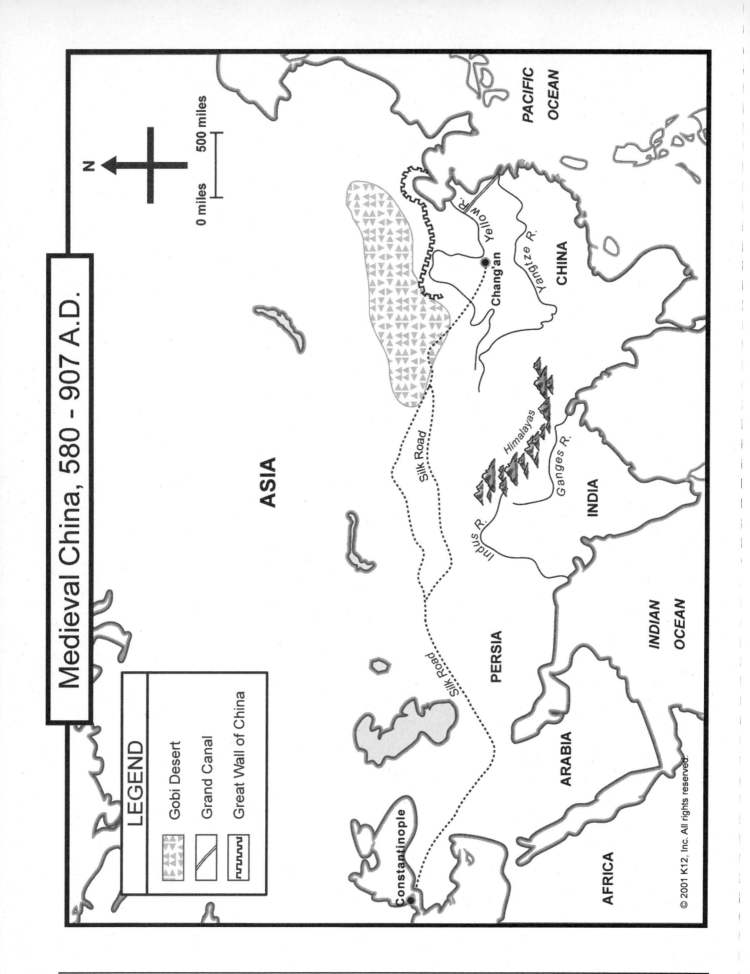

Medieval China, 580 – 907 A.D.

LEGEND

Gobi Desert	
Grand Canal	
Great Wall of China	

N

500 miles

0 miles

PACIFIC OCEAN

ASIA

CHINA

Chang'an

Yellow R.

Yangtze R.

Silk Road

Himalayas

Ganges R.

Indus R.

INDIA

PERSIA

ARABIA

AFRICA

INDIAN OCEAN

Silk Road

Constantinople

Name _____   Date _____

Emperors Rule

Use the word bank to find the words that complete the sentences—write the words in the blanks.
Then write the name of the country inside the outline, and color the three emperors.

There were three emperors in the Sui ruling family. Emperors Wendi, Yangdi,
and Gongdi ruled the large country of _____ at different times.
Together these rulers were called the Sui _____ .

Word Bank

brothers	China	Congo	dynasty

Travel on the Grand Canal

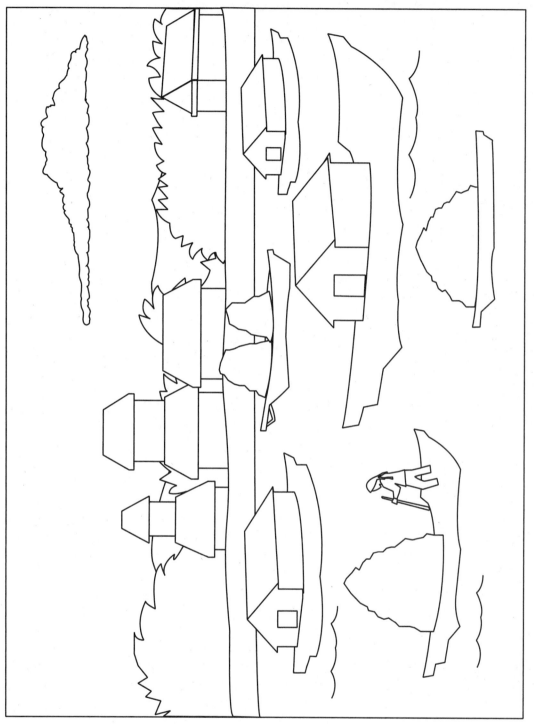

Lesson Assessment

The Grand Canal

1. Locate the Yellow River on your map.

2. Locate the Yangtze River on your map.

3. How did the Chinese emperors solve the problem of taking goods between these two rivers?

4. What was Hua-Mei's barge carrying?

5. What is a dynasty?

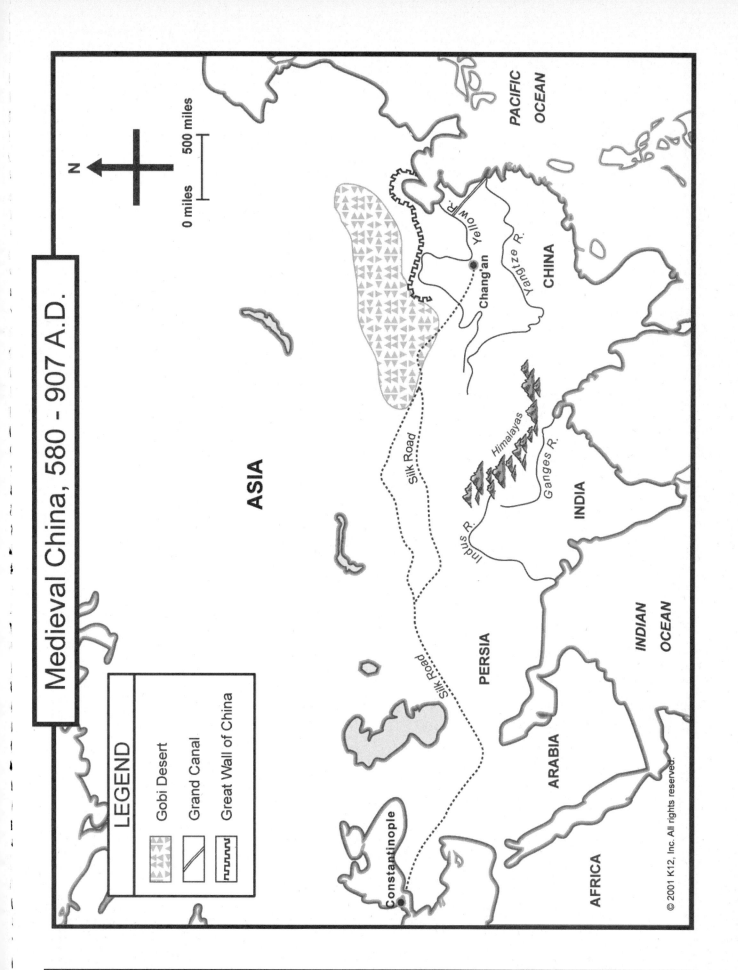

Medieval China, 580 - 907 A.D.

LEGEND

Gobi Desert

Grand Canal

Great Wall of China

N

500 miles

0 miles

PACIFIC OCEAN

ASIA

CHINA

Chang'an

Yellow R.

Yangtze R.

Himalayas

Ganges R.

Indus R.

INDIA

PERSIA

ARABIA

AFRICA

INDIAN OCEAN

Constantinople

Silk Road

Silk Road

© 2001 K12, Inc. All rights reserved.

Student Guide
Lesson 3: Buddhism in China

Lesson Objectives

- Demonstrate mastery of important knowledge and skills taught in previous lessons.
- State that Buddhism is a religion that began in India and became important in China.
- State that Buddhism is based on the teachings of Buddha.

PREPARE

Approximate lesson time is 60 minutes.

Materials

For the Student
- 🖥 map of Medieval China

Optional
- 🖥 A Buddhist Temple in China activity sheet
- 🖥 What Did Buddha Teach? activity sheet

map, world

pencils, no. 2

paper, 8 1/2" x 11"

pencils, colored, 16 or more

crayons, 16 or more

Buddha Stories compiled and illustrated by Demi

Keywords and Pronunciation

Buddha (BOO-duh)
Buddhism (BOO-dih-zuhm)
Chang´an (chahng-en)
Xuanzang (shoo-en-dzawng)

LEARN
Activity 1: Great Structures Review (Online)

Activity 2: Meet Xuanzang (Online)

Activity 3: Show You Know *(Online)*

Activity 4: History Record Book *(Online)*

Activity 5. Optional: A Buddhist Temple in China *(Online)*

Activity 6. Optional: What Did Buddha Teach? *(Online)*

ASSESS

Lesson Assessment: Buddhism in China (*Online*)

You will complete an offline assessment covering the main objectives of this lesson. Your learning coach will score this assessment.

LEARN

Activity 7. Optional: Buddha Stories *(Online)*

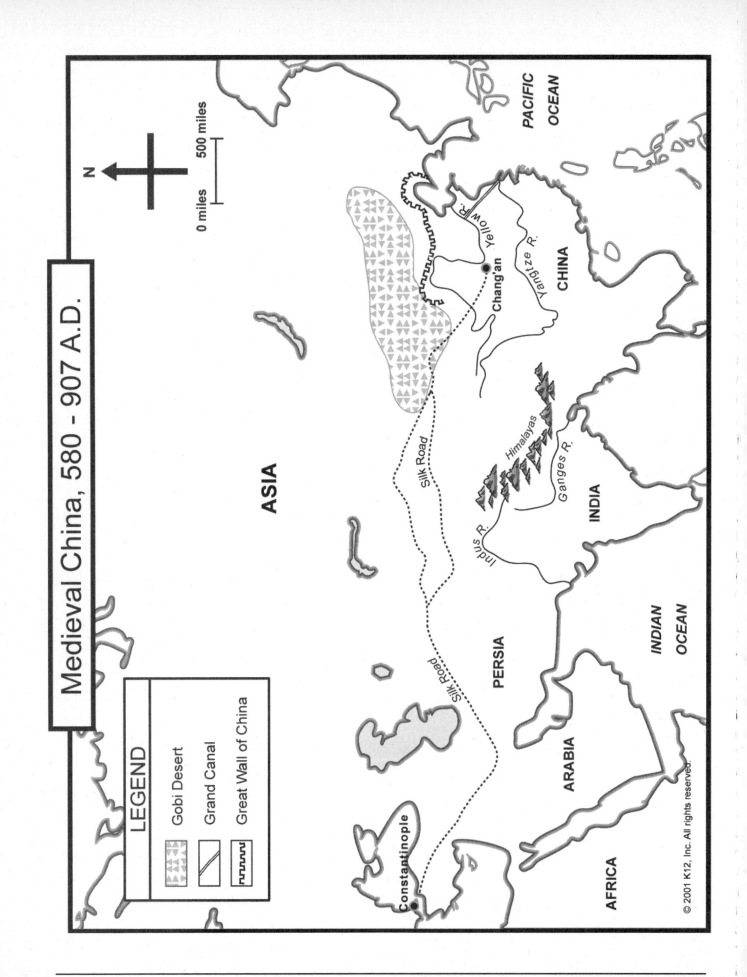

Medieval China, 580 – 907 A.D.

LEGEND

Gobi Desert

Grand Canal

Great Wall of China

ASIA

PACIFIC OCEAN

CHINA

Chang'an

Yellow R.

Yangtze R.

Silk Road

Himalayas

Ganges R.

Indus R.

INDIA

PERSIA

ARABIA

AFRICA

INDIAN OCEAN

Silk Road

Constantinople

N

500 miles

0 miles

Name

Date

What Did Buddha Teach?

Read the statements under the statue of Buddha. Cross out the ones that say things Buddha did *not* teach. Then color the statue.

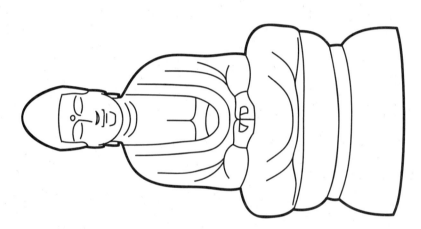

1. Buddha taught that living a good life meant trying to act the right way.

2. Buddha taught that people should not eat meat and fish.

3. Buddha taught people to wear special clothing and shoes.

4. Buddha taught people that wanting too many things would make them unhappy.

5. Buddha taught people to be kind to all living creatures.

Name

Date

A Buddhist Temple in China

Color this Buddhist temple. Then fill in the blanks below. Draw your own statue of Buddha on the back if you want.

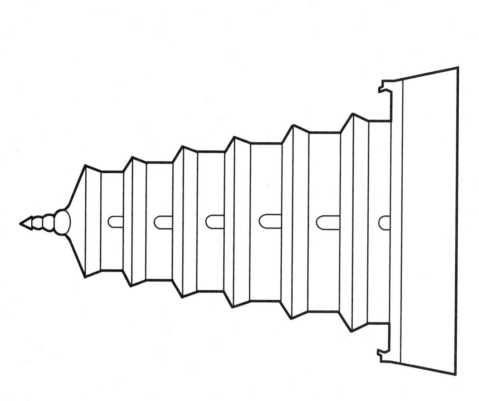

This is a Buddhist place of worship called a _____ .

Inside there is a statue of _____ .

Lesson Assessment

Buddhism in China

1. Did Buddhism begin in India or China?

2. What do people call the teacher who began Buddhism?

3. Did many people in China become Buddhists, or just a few?

Student Guide
Lesson 4: The Trading Tang: The Silk Road

Lesson Objectives

- Demonstrate mastery of important knowledge and skills taught in previous lessons.
- Locate the Silk Road on a map.
- Explain that the Tang dynasty encouraged trade.
- Identify the Silk Road as a great overland trade route between Europe and Asia.

PREPARE

Approximate lesson time is 60 minutes.

Materials

For the Student

   💻 map of Medieval China

Optional

   💻 Traveling the Silk Road activity sheet

  map, world

  pencils, no. 2

  paper, 8 1/2" x 11"

  pencils, colored, 16 or more

  clay, colored

  crayons, 16 or more

  markers, colored, 8 or more

  Stories from the Silk Road by Cherry Gilchrist

  The Silk Route: 7000 Miles of History by John S. Major

Keywords and Pronunciation

Chang´an (chahng-en)

Hafez (hah-FEZ)

Samir (suh-MEER)

Xuanzang (shoo-en-dzawng)

LEARN
Activity 1: Review of China (Online)

Activity 2: Journeys Across the Silk Road (Online)

Activity 3: Show You Know (Online)

Activity 4: History Record Book (Online)

Activity 5. Optional: The Tang Dynasty Encourages Trade (Online)

Activity 6. Optional: Traveling the Silk Road (Online)

ASSESS

Lesson Assessment: The Trading Tang: The Silk Road (*Online*)

You will complete an offline assessment covering the main objectives of this lesson. Your learning coach will score this assessment.

LEARN

Activity 7. Optional: Silk Road Stories (Online)

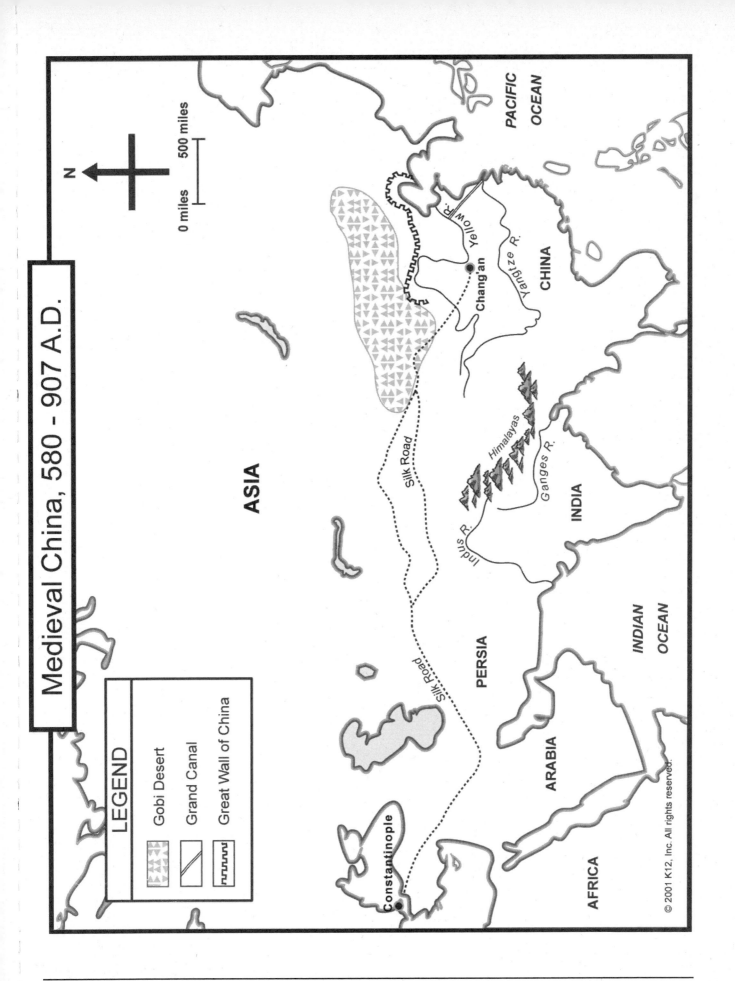

Medieval China, 580 – 907 A.D.

LEGEND

Gobi Desert	
Grand Canal	
Great Wall of China	

N

500 miles

0 miles

PACIFIC
OCEAN

Yellow R.

Chang'an

Yangtze R.

CHINA

Himalayas

Ganges R.

Indus R.

INDIA

ASIA

Silk Road

PERSIA

Silk Road

ARABIA

AFRICA

INDIAN
OCEAN

Constantinople

Traveling the Silk Road

Color the rivers, seas and ocean blue. Color everything else in the colors of your choice.

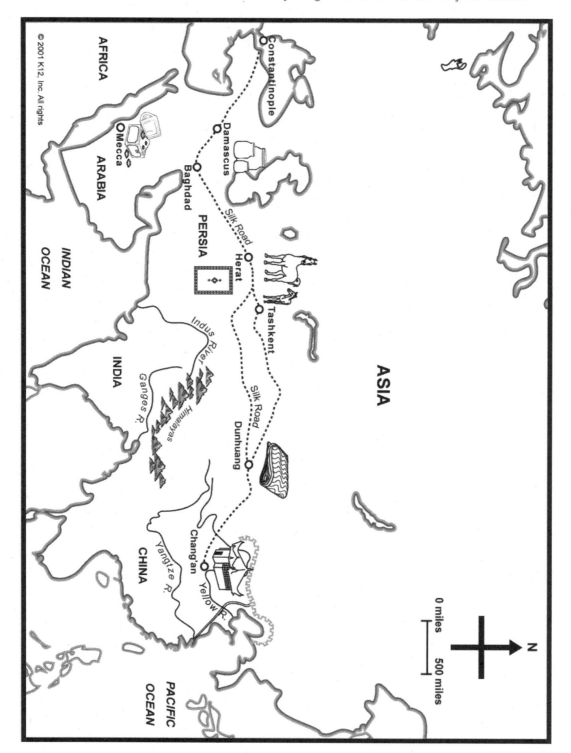

Lesson Assessment

The Trading Tang: The Silk Road

1. Where is the Silk Road on your map?

2. Which two continents does it travel through?

3. Why was the Silk Road important to China and other lands during medieval times?

4. What was the name of the dynasty that made the Silk Road safe for merchants and brought more trade to China?

5. How was the Silk Road made safe for merchants?

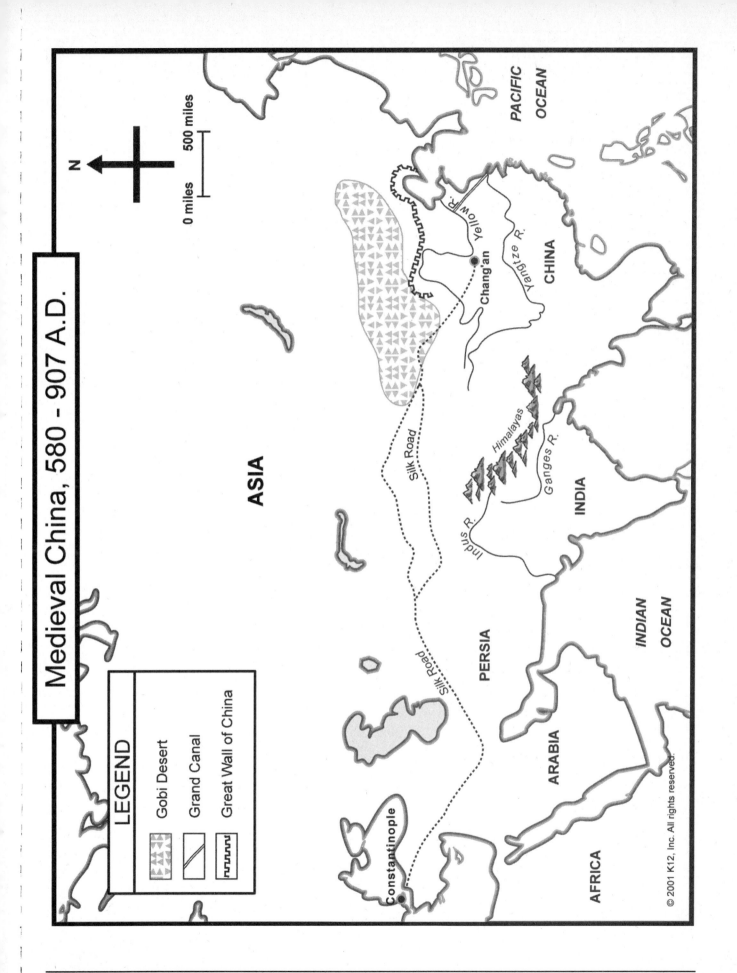

Medieval China, 580 - 907 A.D.

N

500 miles

0 miles

LEGEND

	Gobi Desert
	Grand Canal
	Great Wall of China

ASIA

PACIFIC OCEAN

CHINA

Yellow R.

Chang'an

Yangtze R.

Himalayas

Ganges R.

Indus R.

INDIA

Silk Road

PERSIA

INDIAN OCEAN

ARABIA

AFRICA

Constantinople

Silk Road

Student Guide
Lesson 5: Mulan

Lesson Objectives
- Demonstrate mastery of important knowledge and skills taught in previous lessons.
- Identify Mulan as a Chinese heroine.
- State that *The Song of Mulan* is a story about a young woman who disguises herself as a man and fights with the Chinese army against invaders.

PREPARE

Approximate lesson time is 60 minutes.

Materials
For the Student
- 🖳 map of Medieval China

Optional
- 🖳 All About Mulan activity sheet
  - pencils, no. 2
  - paper, 8 1/2" x 11"
  - pencils, colored, 16 or more
  - paints, watercolor, 8 colors or more
  - paper, drawing, 12" x 18"
  - Fa Mulan: The Story of a Woman Warrior by Robert D. San Souci

Keywords and Pronunciation
Mulan (moo-lan)

LEARN
Activity 1: Roads and Walls *(Online)*

Activity 2: The Story of Mulan *(Online)*

Activity 3: Show You Know *(Online)*

Activity 4: History Record Book *(Online)*

Activity 5. Optional: All About Mulan Puzzle *(Online)*

Activity 6. Optional: A Poem of Mulan *(Online)*

ASSESS

Lesson Assessment: Mulan (*Online*)

You will complete an offline assessment covering the main objectives of this lesson. Your learning coach will score this assessment.

LEARN

Activity 7. Optional: *Fa Mulan* *(Online)*

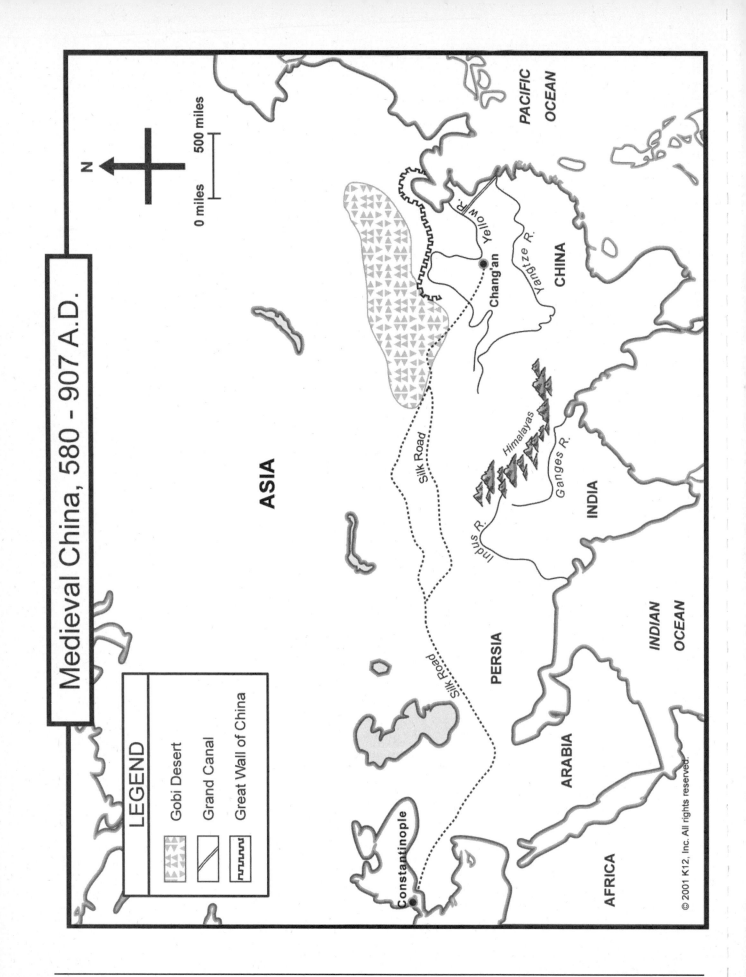

Medieval China, 580 – 907 A.D.

LEGEND

Gobi Desert

Grand Canal

Great Wall of China

N

500 miles

0 miles

PACIFIC OCEAN

CHINA

Chang'an

Yellow R.

Yangtze R.

ASIA

Silk Road

Himalayas

Ganges R.

Indus R.

INDIA

PERSIA

ARABIA

INDIAN OCEAN

AFRICA

Silk Road

Constantinople

All About Mulan

Read the questions and fill out the crossword puzzle below.

Across
2. fighter
6. name of one ruling family
7. leader of soldiers
10. ruler
12. girl child
13. ruling family

Down
1. woman who is head of a family
3. famous Chinese road
4. man who is head of a family
5. Chinese River
8. person who makes cloth
9. Chinese heroine
11. Asian country

Lesson Assessment

Mulan

1. What is the name of the brave Chinese heroine we read about?

2. What is The Song of Mulan?

3. What does the story say about how Mulan was able to take her father's place?

4. What happened in the story after Mulan took her father's place?

Student Guide
Lesson 6: The Inventive Song Dynasty

Lesson Objectives
Demonstrate mastery of important knowledge and skills taught in previous lessons.

• Identify and explain the functions of any two of these inventions that came during the Song dynasty: the compass, paper money, gunpowder, and movable type.

• Recognize that the Song dynasty was a time of invention in China.

PREPARE
Approximate lesson time is 60 minutes.

Materials
For the student

    pens, no. 2

    paper, 8 1/2" x 11"

    pencil, colored, 16 or more

Optional

    paper, drawing, 12" x 18" (2)

    Made in China by Suzanne Williams

Keywords and Pronunciation
Song (soong)

LEARN
Activity 1: Mulan and More *(Online)*

Activity 2: Great Inventions of the Song *(Online)*

Activity 3: Show You Know *(Online)*

Activity 4: History Record Book *(Online)*

Activity 5. Optional: The Riddles of Song *(Online)*

Activity 6. Optional: Inventions Then and Now (Online)

ASSESS

Lesson Assessment: The Inventive Song Dynasty (Online)

You will complete an offline assessment covering the main objectives of this lesson. Your learning coach will score this assessment.

LEARN

Activity 7. Optional: Made in China (Online)

Lesson Assessment

The Inventive Song Dynasty

1. What was the Song dynasty famous for?

2. Name two inventions from the time of the Song dynasty.

3. Answer at least two of the following: What did people use the compass for? What was something that people used gunpowder for? Why was movable type an important invention? How did paper money help the Chinese?

Student Guide
Lesson 7. Optional: A Very Important Test

Lesson Objectives

- Identify civil service examinations as tests people took to get jobs in government.
- Explain that scholars were honored in medieval China.
- State that Song rulers wanted scholars to help run the government.
- Demonstrate mastery of important knowledge and skills taught in previous lessons.

PREPARE

Approximate lesson time is 60 minutes.

Materials

For the Student
Optional

    📖 A Chinese Scholar activity sheet

    pencils, no. 2

    paper, 8 1/2" x 11"

    pencils, colored, 16 or more

    glue sticks

    paper, colored construction, 12"x12"

    scissors, round-end safety

    crayons, 16 or more

    Ancient China by Arthur Cotterell

Keywords and Pronunciation

scholar : A person who loves to learn.

Wang Yu (wahng yee)

LEARN
Activity 1. Optional: Optional Lesson Instructions *(Online)*

This lesson is OPTIONAL. It is provided for students who seek enrichment or extra practice. You may skip this lesson.

If you choose to skip this lesson, then go to the Plan or Lesson Lists page and mark this lesson "Skipped" in order to proceed to the next lesson in the course.

Activity 2. Optional: China Review *(Online)*

Activity 3. Optional: A Test for Scholars *(Online)*

Activity 4. Optional: Show You Know *(Online)*

Activity 5. Optional: History Record Book *(Online)*

Activity 6. Optional: Wang Yu's Path to the Palace *(Online)*

Activity 7. Optional: Looking Scholarly *(Online)*

Activity 8. Optional: An Eyewitness to Ancient China *(Online)*

Name _____   Date _____

A Chinese Scholar

Color this picture of a Chinese scholar. He has been studying for his civil service test. Write a caption about his studies.

_____

_____

_____

Student Guide
Lesson 8: Mongols on the March: Genghis Khan

Lesson Objectives
- Demonstrate mastery of important knowledge and skills taught in previous lessons.
- Identify Genghis Khan as the founder of the Mongol Empire.
- State that Genghis Khan invaded China.

PREPARE

Approximate lesson time is 60 minutes.

Materials
For the Student

    🖥 map of the Mongol Empire

    History Record Book

    pencils, no. 2

    paper, 8 1/2" x 11"

    pencils, colored, 16 or more

Keywords and Pronunciation
Genghis Khan (GENG-guhs KAHN)
Mongols (MAHNG-guhls)
Temujen (TEM-yuh-juhn)

LEARN
Activity 1: China and More *(Online)*

Activity 2: The Unbeatable Prince *(Online)*

Activity 3: Show You Know *(Online)*

Activity 4: History Record Book *(Online)*

Activity 5. Optional: What's in a Name? *(Online)*

ASSESS

Lesson Assessment: Mongols on the March: Genghis Khan (*Online*)

You will complete an offline assessment covering the main objectives of this lesson. Your learning coach will score this assessment.

LEARN

Activity 6. Optional: Virtual Khan (*Online*)

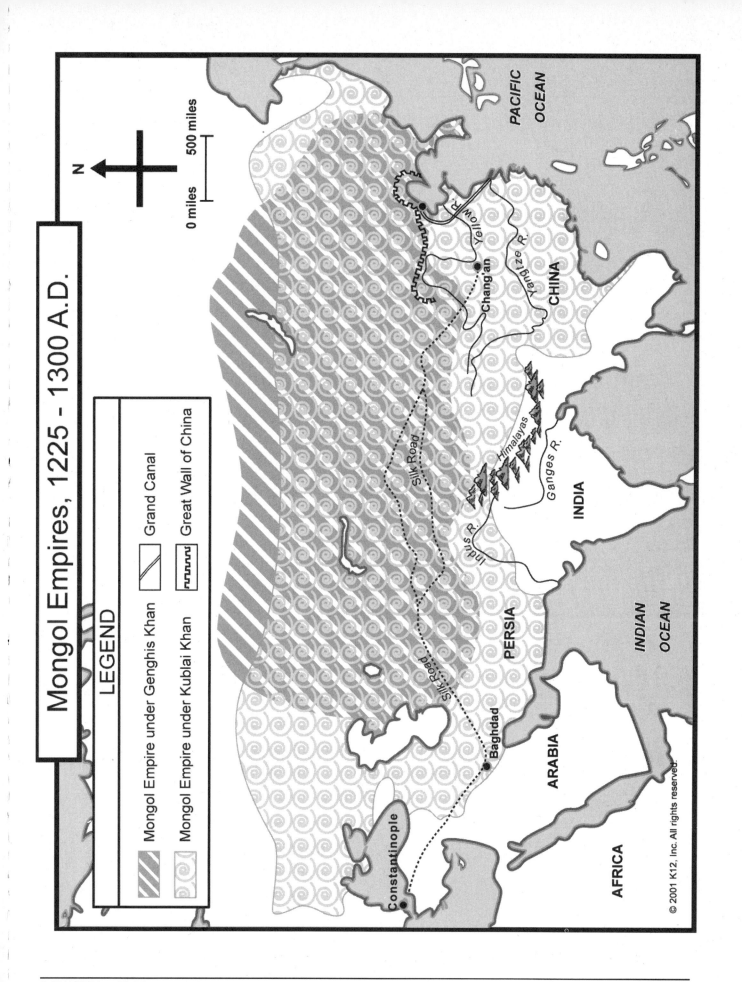

Mongol Empires, 1225 – 1300 A.D.

LEGEND

Mongol Empire under Genghis Khan

Mongol Empire under Kublai Khan

Grand Canal

Great Wall of China

500 miles

0 miles

N

PACIFIC OCEAN

Yellow R.

Chang'an

Yangtze R.

CHINA

Himalayas

Ganges R.

INDIA

Indus R.

Silk Road

Silk Road

PERSIA

Baghdad

ARABIA

INDIAN OCEAN

AFRICA

Constantinople

© 2001 K12, Inc. All rights reserved.

Lesson Assessment

Mongols on the March: Genghis Khan

1. Who was the leader of the Mongols and the founder of the Mongol Empire?

2. Genghis Khan led his army south and invaded a great Asian empire. Which empire was that?

Student Guide
Lesson 9: Kublai Khan

Lesson Objectives

- Demonstrate mastery of important knowledge and skills taught in previous lessons.
- State that the Mongols conquered all of China.
- Identify Kublai Khan as the first Mongol emperor of China.

PREPARE

Approximate lesson time is 60 minutes.

Materials

For the Student
- 🖥 map of the Mongol Empire

Optional
- 🖥 Inside the Palace activity sheet
- 🖥 Kublai Khan in Action activity sheet
- pencils, no. 2
- paper, 8 1/2" x 11"
- pencils, colored, 16 or more
- crayons, 16 or more

Keywords and Pronunciation

Beijing (bay-zhing)
Kublai Khan (KOO-bluh KAHN)
Yuan (you-EN)

LEARN
Activity 1: Review *(Online)*

Activity 2: Kublai Khan Expands the Empire *(Online)*

Activity 3: Show You Know *(Online)*

Activity 4: History Record Book *(Online)*

Activity 5. Optional: Inside Kublai Khan's Yuan Dynasty *(Online)*

Activity 6. Optional: Kublai Khan in Action *(Online)*

ASSESS

Lesson Assessment: Kublai Khan (*Offline*)

You will complete an offline assessment covering the main objectives of this lesson. Your learning coach will score this assessment.

LEARN

Activity 7. Optional: The Beijing Opera, A Legacy of the Yuan *(Online)*

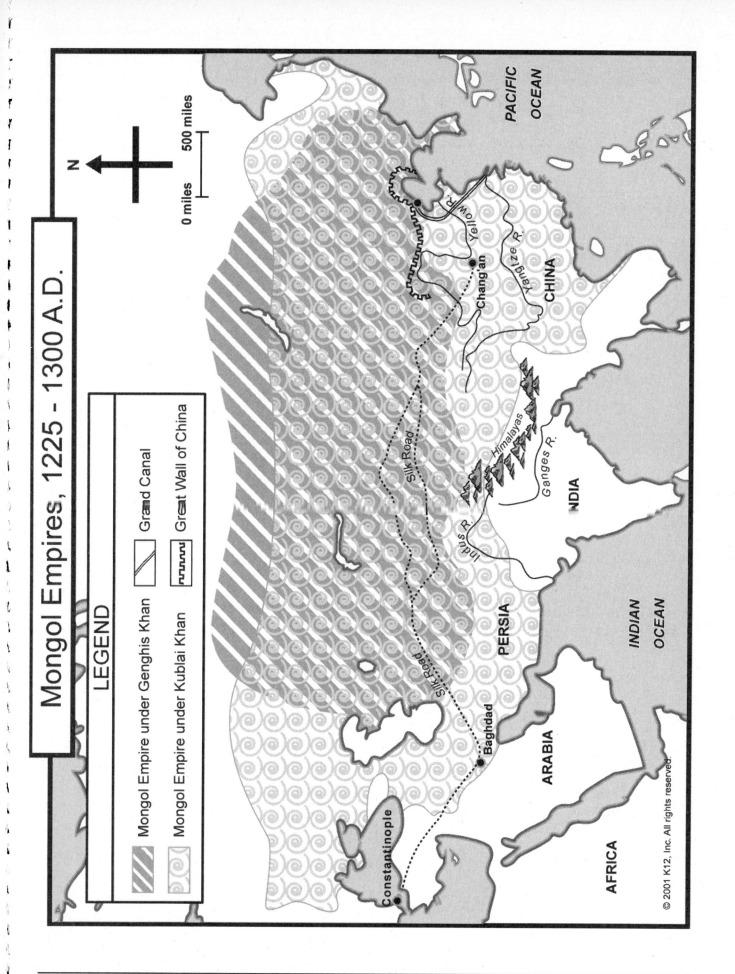

Mongol Empires, 1225 – 1300 A.D.

LEGEND

Grand Canal

Great Wall of China

Mongol Empire under Genghis Khan

Mongol Empire under Kublai Khan

N

500 miles

0 miles

PACIFIC OCEAN

Yellow R.

Chang'an

Yangtze R.

CHINA

Himalayas

Ganges R.

Indus R.

INDIA

Silk Road

PERSIA

Baghdad

ARABIA

INDIAN OCEAN

AFRICA

Silk Road

Constantinople

Name   Date

Kublai Khan in Action

Color Kublai Khan in action. Use colors that show the power of Kublai Khan.

Name _____   Date _____

Inside the Palace

This is a drawing of Kublai Khan's palace. Fill the inside with words or drawings that tell what he did while starting the Yuan dynasty.

Lesson Assessment

Kublai Khan

1. What people conquered all of China during the Middle Ages?

2. What was the name of Genghis Khan's grandson who became the first Mongol emperor of China?

Student Guide
Lesson 10: Marco Polo: Man of a Million Stories

Lesson Objectives
- Demonstrate mastery of important knowledge and skills taught in previous lessons.
- Identify Marco Polo as a famous traveler and explorer.
- Explain that Marco Polo traveled from Venice to China and its large empire.
- State that Marco Polo worked for Kublai Khan in China.

PREPARE

Approximate lesson time is 60 minutes.

Materials
For the Student
Optional
    📖 map of Marco Polo's Journey
    pencils, no. 2
    paper, 8 1/2" x 11"
    pencils, colored, 16 or more
    1-hole punch
    crayons, 16 or more
    glue sticks
    paper, colored construction, 12"x12"
    Marco Polo: A Journey Through China by Fiona MacDonald

Keywords and Pronunciation
Gobi (GOH-bee)
Marco Polo (MAHR-koh POH-loh)
Pamir (puh-MEER)

LEARN
Activity 1: The Khans (Online)

Activity 2: Marco Polo in China (Online)

Activity 3: Show You Know *(Online)*

Activity 4: History Record Book *(Online)*

Activity 5. Optional: A Treasure Map of Marco Polo's Adventures *(Online)*

Activity 6. Optional: Marco Polo: Hall of Fame Traveler *(Online)*

ASSESS

Lesson Assessment: Marco Polo: Man of a Million Stories (*Online*)

You will complete an offline assessment covering the main objectives of this lesson. Your learning coach will score this assessment.

LEARN
Activity 7. Optional: A Journey Through China *(Online)*

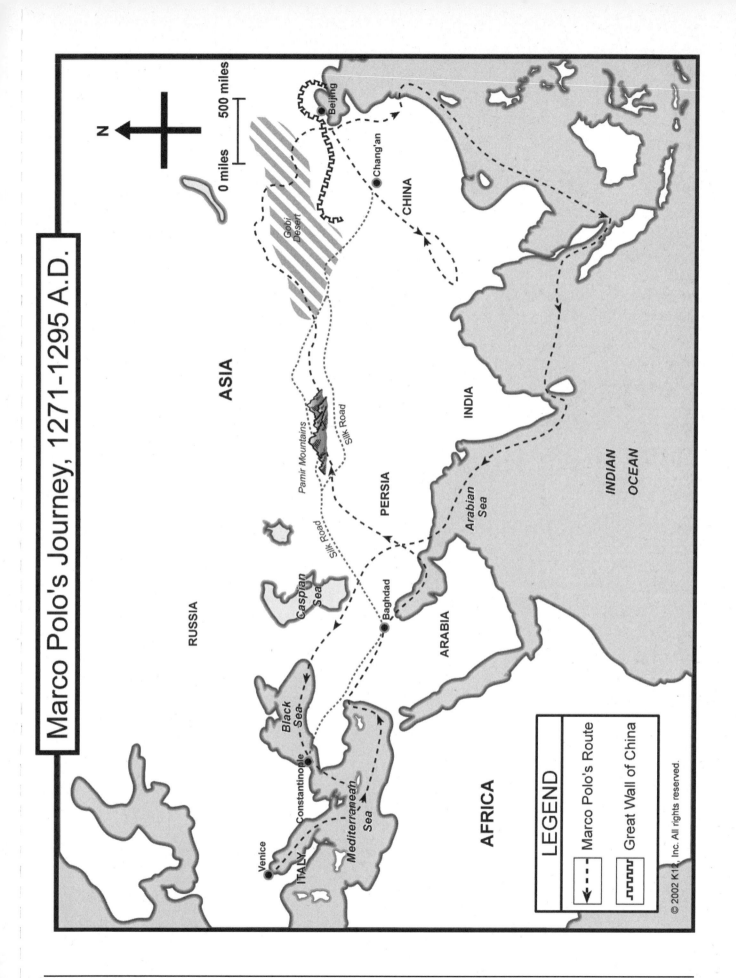

Marco Polo's Journey, 1271–1295 A.D.

N

500 miles

0 miles

Beijing

Chang'an

CHINA

Gobi Desert

ASIA

Pamir Mountains

Silk Road

INDIA

Silk Road

Caspian Sea

PERSIA

Arabian Sea

INDIAN OCEAN

RUSSIA

Baghdad

ARABIA

Black Sea

Constantinople

ITALY

Venice

Mediterranean Sea

AFRICA

LEGEND

Marco Polo's Route

Great Wall of China

Lesson Assessment

Marco Polo: Man of a Million Stories

1. What is the name of the famous traveler we learned about?

2. Why was Marco Polo famous?

3. Where did Marco Polo begin his travels, and where did he go?

4. What was the name of the Chinese emperor Marco Polo worked for?

Student Guide
Lesson 11: China Makes China: Porcelain

Lesson Objectives

- Demonstrate mastery of important knowledge and skills taught in previous lessons.
- Identify porcelain as a fine pottery invented in China.
- Explain that the English word "china" for dishes comes from the fact that the Chinese invented porcelain.
- Demonstrate mastery of important knowledge and skills in this unit.
- Identify Confucius as a great Chinese teacher.
- Identify the Grand Canal as a long, man-made waterway in China.
- State that Buddhism is a religion that began in India and became important in China.
- Identify the Silk Road as a great overland trade route between Europe and Asia.
- Identify and explain the functions of any two of these inventions that came during the Song dynasty: the compass, paper money, gunpowder, and movable type.
- Identify Genghis Khan as the founder of the Mongol Empire.
- Identify Kublai Khan as the first Mongol emperor of China.
- Explain that Marco Polo traveled from Venice to China and its large empire.

PREPARE

Approximate lesson time is 60 minutes.

Materials

For the Student

    🖥 map of Marco Polo's Journey

Optional

      clay, colored

      toothpicks

Keywords and Pronunciation

Han Yi (hahn yee)

porcelain : Hard, fine, white ceramic ware, also called china.

Wu Hong (woo hohng)

LEARN
Activity 1: A Return to Marco Polo *(Online)*

Activity 2: Dreaming of Dragons *(Online)*

Activity 3. Optional: More Dragons *(Online)*

Activity 4. Optional: China's China *(Online)*

Activity 5: History Record Book Review *(Online)*

ASSESS

Unit Assessment: Medieval China (*Offline*)

Complete an offline Unit Assessment. Your learning coach will score this part of the Assessment.

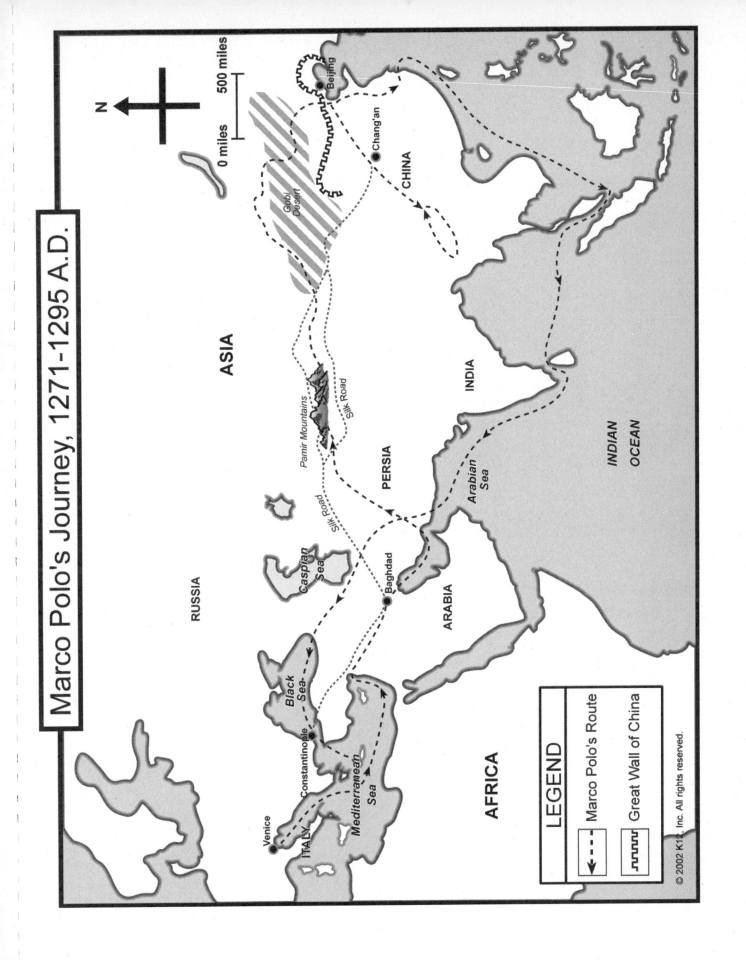

Marco Polo's Journey, 1271-1295 A.D.

N

500 miles
0 miles

ASIA

RUSSIA

Beijing

Gobi Desert

Chang'an

CHINA

Pamir Mountains

Silk Road

Silk Road

Caspian Sea

INDIA

PERSIA

Arabian Sea

Baghdad

ARABIA

INDIAN OCEAN

Black Sea

Constantinople

Venice

ITALY

Mediterranean Sea

AFRICA

LEGEND

- - - ▼ Marco Polo's Route

ⴖⴖⴖ Great Wall of China

© 2002 K12, Inc. All rights reserved.

Name _____   Date _____

Medieval China

Read each sentence and its answer choices. Fill in the bubble in front of the word or words that best answer the question.

1. Why is the finely made pottery called porcelain also known as "china"?
   - ○ The Chinese captured the inventor.
   - ○ The Chinese bought the right to name it that.
   - ○ The Chinese invented it.

2. Who was a great Chinese teacher?
   - ○ Mansa Musa
   - ○ Marco Polo
   - ○ Confucius

3. What was the name of the man-made waterway built to connect the Yellow and Yangtze Rivers?
   - ○ the Panama Canal
   - ○ the Grand Canal
   - ○ the Yalu Connector

4. What religion began in India and later became important in China?
   - ○ Christianity
   - ○ Judaism
   - ○ Buddhism

5. What is the name of the overland trade route that connected Asia and Europe?
   - ○ the Silk Road
   - ○ the Tang Trail
   - ○ the China Highway

6. Who was the first Mongol emperor of China?
   - ○ Confucius
   - ○ Kublai Khan
   - ○ Mansa Musa

7. Which of these Chinese inventions helped people, especially sailors, find their way?
   - ○ compass
   - ○ movable type
   - ○ gunpowder

8. During which dynasty were paper money, compasses, and fireworks invented?
   - ○ Song
   - ○ Chin
   - ○ Han

9. What traveler and explorer left his home in Venice and spent twenty years traveling to China and other parts of Asia?
   - ○ Sundiata
   - ○ Mulan
   - ○ Marco Polo

10. Who was the founder of the Mongol Empire?
    - ○ Genghis Khan
    - ○ Immanuel Kant
    - ○ Hari Khan

Student Guide
Lesson 1: Japan: The Island Kingdom

Travel back to feudal Japan, where Shinto and Buddhism had become important religions. Meet shoguns, daimyos, and samurai warriors. Learn how the people of feudal Japan lived and acted. Then discover how China's Kublai Khan attempted to invade Japan and was foiled by a typhoon.

Lesson Objectives

- Locate the Pacific Ocean on a map.
- Locate Japan on a map.
- State that Japan has four main islands.
- Name Mount Fuji as the biggest volcano in Japan.
- Define an archipelago as a group of islands.

PREPARE

Approximate lesson time is 60 minutes.

Materials

For the Student

    🖥 map of Medieval Japan

Optional

    🖥 Japanese Geography activity sheet

    map, world

    crayons, 16 or more

    pencils, no. 2

    paper, 8 1/2" x 11"

    pencils, colored, 16 or more

    pan, baking

    banana

    gelatin - blue

Keywords and Pronunciation

archipelago (ahr-kuh-PEH-luh-goh) : A group of islands.

Fuji (FOO-jee)

Hokkaido (hoh-KIY-doh)

Honshu (HAWN-shoo)

Izanagi (iz-ah-nah-GEE)

Izanami (iz-ah-nah-MEE)

Kyushu (KYOO-shoo)

Shikoku (shee-KOH-koo)

LEARN
Activity 1: Middle Ages Everywhere *(Online)*

Activity 2: Mysterious Japan *(Online)*

Activity 3: Show You Know *(Online)*

Activity 4: History Record Book *(Online)*

Activity 5. Optional: Japanese Geography *(Online)*

ASSESS

Lesson Assessment: Japan: The Island Kingdom (*Online*)
You will complete an offline assessment covering the main objectives of this lesson. Your learning coach will score this assessment.

LEARN
Activity 6. Optional: The Japanese Archipelago As Food *(Online)*

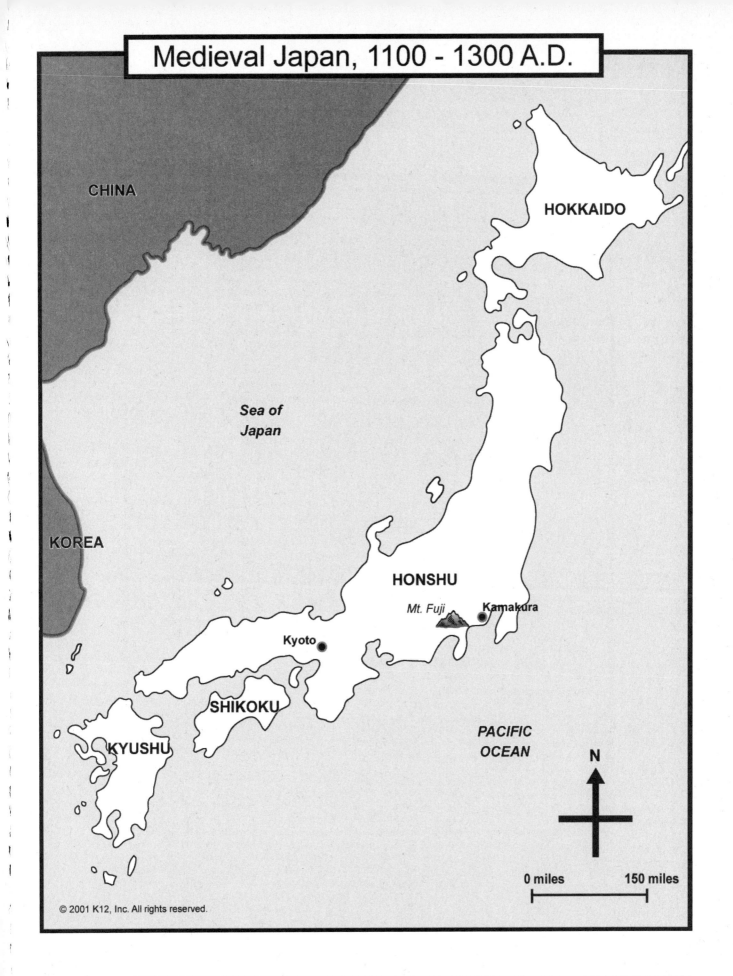

Medieval Japan, 1100 - 1300 A.D.

CHINA

HOKKAIDO

Sea of
Japan

KOREA

HONSHU

Mt. Fuji Kamakura

Kyoto

SHIKOKU

KYUSHU

PACIFIC
OCEAN

N

0 miles   150 miles

339

Japanese Geography activity sheet

Circle the country of Japan in red. Label the Pacific Ocean in blue. Draw a tiny volcano on the island where Mount Fuji is located. Complete the sentence below.

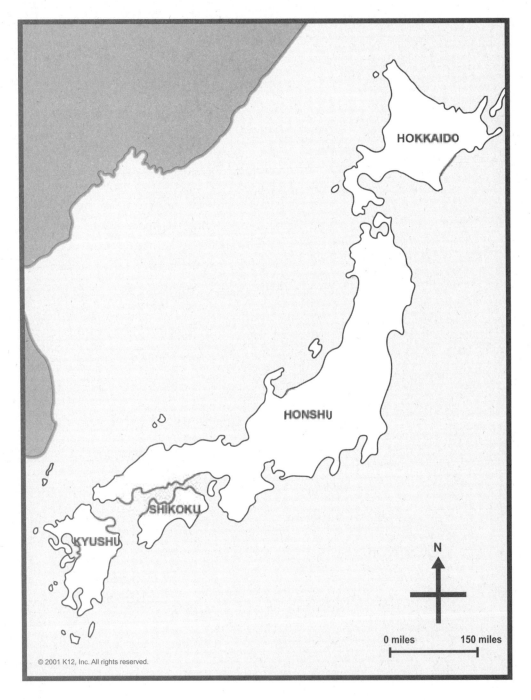

© 2001 K12, Inc. All rights reserved.

Japan is an _____ that is made up of _____ main islands.

Lesson Assessment

Japan: The Island Kingdom

1. Point to Japan on the map.

2. Point to the Pacific Ocean on the map.

3. What is an archipelago?

4. How many major islands does Japan have?

5. What is the name of the biggest volcano in Japan?

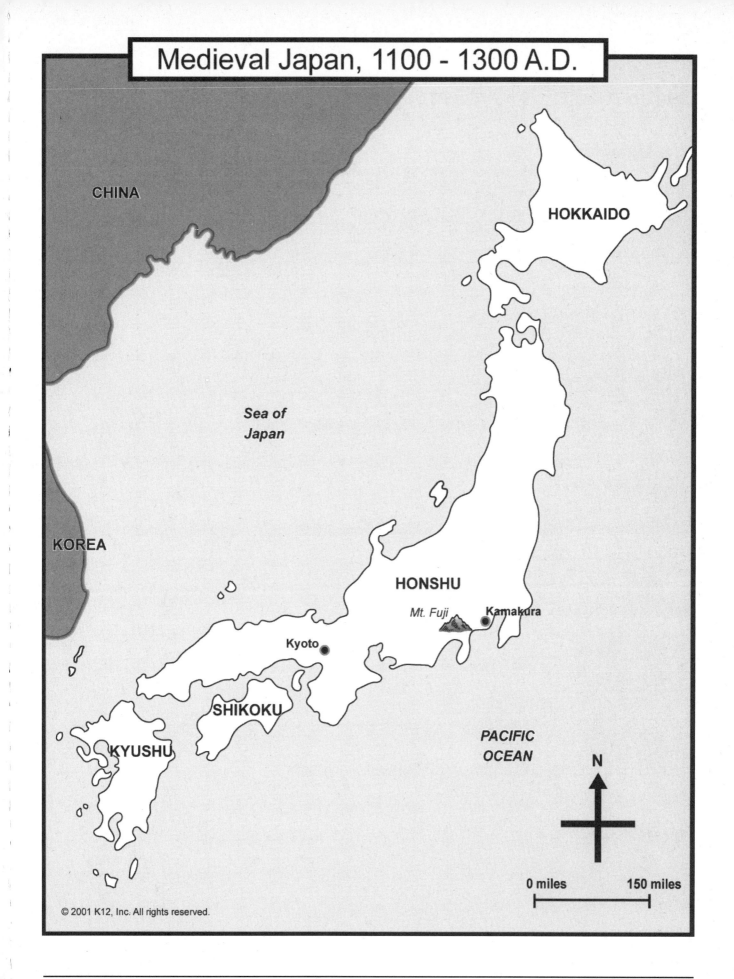

Medieval Japan, 1100 - 1300 A.D.

CHINA

HOKKAIDO

Sea of
Japan

KOREA

HONSHU

Mt. Fuji

Kamakura

Kyoto

SHIKOKU

KYUSHU

*PACIFIC
OCEAN*

N

0 miles   150 miles

© 2001 K12, Inc. All rights reserved.

Student Guide
Lesson 2: Shinto: An Ancient Japanese Religion

Lesson Objectives

- Demonstrate mastery of important knowledge and skills taught in previous lessons.
- State that Shinto is Japan's oldest surviving religion.
- Identify *kami* as Shinto spirits in nature and ancestors.
- Identify the wooden gate, called a torii, as a symbol of Shintoism.

PREPARE

Approximate lesson time is 60 minutes.

Materials

For the Student

    🖳 map of Medieval Japan

Optional

    🖳 Keiko's Morning activity sheet

    map, world

    pencils, no. 2

    paper, 8 1/2" x 11"

    pencils, colored, 16 or more

    The Stonecutter: A Japanese Folktale by Gerald McDermott

Keywords and Pronunciation

kami (kah-mee)

Keiko (KAY-koh)

kimono (kuh-MOH-noh)

Shinto (SHIN-toh)

Shintoism (SHIN-toh-ih-zuhm)

Shintoists (SHIN-toh-ists)

torii (tor-EE-EE)

LEARN
Activity 1: Japanese Geography Review *(Online)*

Activity 2: Shintoism: Ancient Religion of Japan *(Online)*

Activity 3: Show You Know *(Online)*

Activity 4: History Record Book *(Online)*

Activity 5. Optional: Keiko's Morning *(Online)*

ASSESS

Lesson Assessment: Shinto: An Ancient Japanese Religion *(Online)*
You will complete an offline assessment covering the main objectives of this lesson. Your learning coach will score this assessment.

LEARN
Activity 6. Optional: A Japanese Folktale *(Online)*

Medieval Japan, 1100 - 1300 A.D.

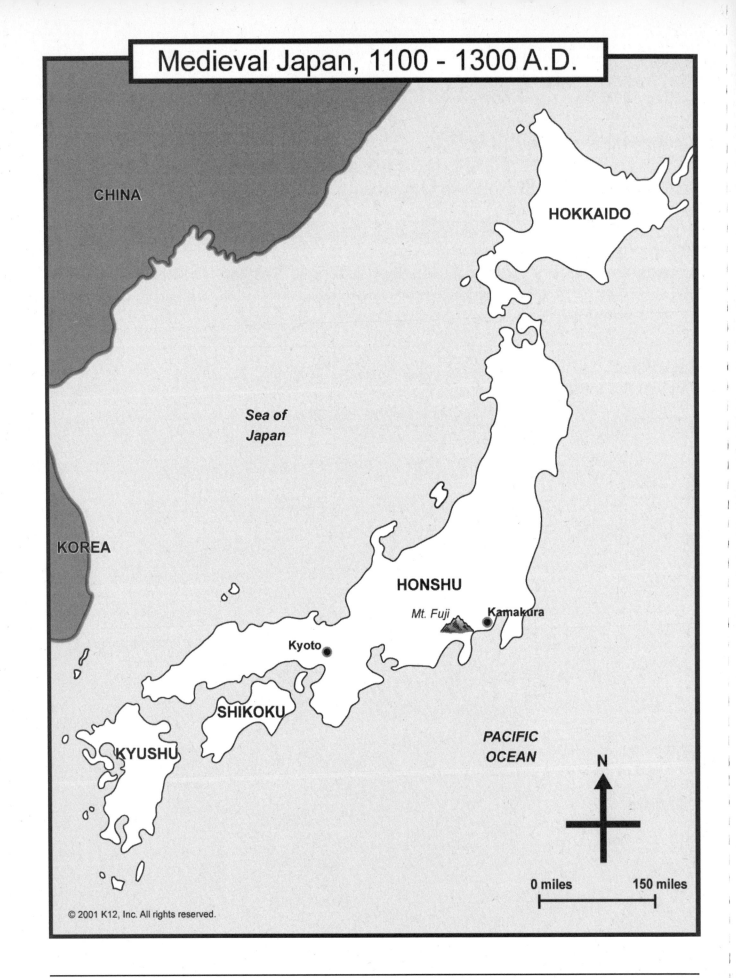

CHINA

HOKKAIDO

Sea of
Japan

KOREA

HONSHU

Mt. Fuji

Kamakura

Kyoto

SHIKOKU

KYUSHU

PACIFIC
OCEAN

N

0 miles   150 miles

Name

Date

Keiko's Morning

Color this picture from the story Keiko's Morning. What is the Japanese word for the wooden gate that is the symbol of Shintoism? Complete the sentence at the bottom.

_____ is Japan's oldest surviving religion.

Lesson Assessment

Shinto: An Ancient Japanese Religion

1. What is the name of the oldest religion in Japan that we know about?

2. Shintoists believe gods and spirits can be found in nature. What are these gods and spirits called?

3. Which of these is a symbol for Shintoism?

Student Guide
Lesson 3: Buddhism in Japan

Lesson Objectives

- Explain that Buddhism came to Japan from China and other parts of Asia.
- Identify the Great Buddha at Kamakura from a photograph.
- Identify a Japanese pagoda from a photograph.

PREPARE

Approximate lesson time is 60 minutes.

Materials

For the Student

Optional

    📖 Buddha Art Photo Album activity sheet

    📖 Religion on the Move activity sheet

    map, world

    pencils, no. 2

    paper, 8 1/2" x 11"

    pencils, colored, 16 or more

    glue sticks

    scissors, round-end safety

    crayons, 16 or more

    cups, plastic

    brush, watercolor

    paints, watercolor, 8 colors or more

    water

Keywords and Pronunciation

Kamakura (kah-mah-KOOR-ah)

pagoda : A Japanese tower erected as a temple and having several stories with roofs curving upward where each story meets.

pagodas (puh-GOH-duhz)

sansui (SAHN-soo-ee)

LEARN
Activity 1: Looking Back at Buddhism (Online)

Activity 2: Gifts from Across the Sea (*Online*)

Activity 3: Buddhist Art from Japan (*Online*)

Activity 4: Show You Know (*Online*)

Activity 5: History Record Book (*Online*)

Activity 6. Optional: Buddha Art Photo Album (*Online*)

Activity 7. Optional: Religion on the Move (*Online*)

ASSESS

Lesson Assessment: Buddhism in Japan (*Online*)

You will complete an offline assessment covering the main objectives of this lesson. Your learning coach will score this assessment.

LEARN

Activity 8. Optional: Landscape Painting (*Online*)

Name _____   Date _____

Buddha Art Photo Album

Color the pictures on the other page, cut them out, and glue them on this page where they belong.

Some Buddha statues are quite large. Here's the Great Buddha at Kamakura - he's 37 feet tall!

Here's a pagoda. The Japanese built these as temples out of wood. Look how the roofs at each floor curve upward!

Here's a photograph of a painting. Japanese artists are famous for their landscape paintings.

Buddha Art Photo Album

✂ cut

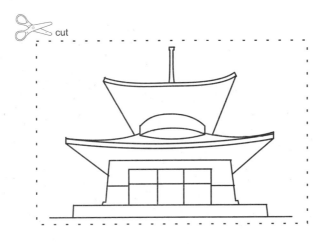

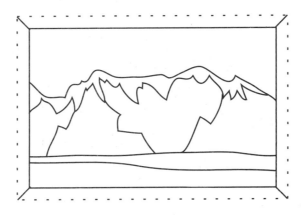

Name _____   **Date** _____

Religion on the Move

Show where Buddhism in Japan came from by drawing two large arrows on the map below. The arrows should start in the area from where it came and point to Japan. Add an arrow symbol to the legend with "path of Buddhism" next to it.

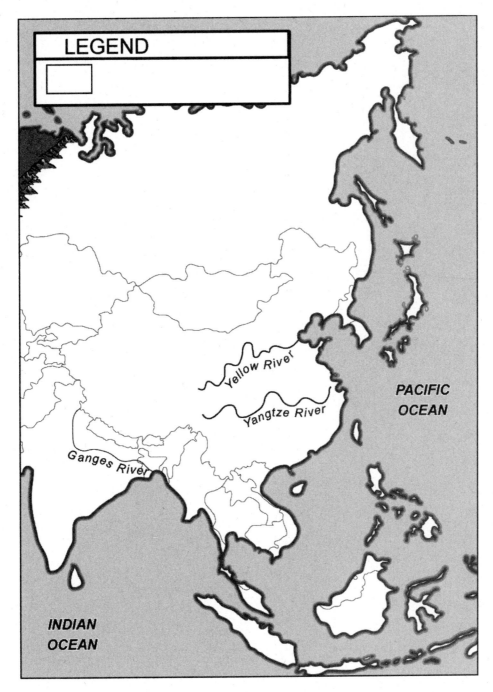

Lesson Assessment

Buddhism in Japan

1. Where did Buddhism in Japan come from?_____

2. What is this statue called?_____

3. What is the name of this kind of building?_____

Student Guide
Lesson 4: Feudal Japan

Lesson Objectives
- Demonstrate mastery of important knowledge and skills taught in previous lessons.
- Define a *shogun* as the commander of the army and real ruler of feudal Japan.
- Define a *daimyo* as a person who owned a lot of land in feudal Japan.
- Identify a Japanese castle from a photograph.

PREPARE

Approximate lesson time is 60 minutes.

Materials
    For the Student
    Optional
        🖥 Japanese Castle activity sheet
      map, world
      pencils, no. 2
      paper, 8 1/2" x 11"
      pencils, colored, 16 or more
      tablets, wide-line handwriting
      A Samurai Castle by Fiona MacDonald

Keywords and Pronunciation
daimyo (DIY-mee-oh) : A baron in feudal Japan.
daimyos (DIY-mee-ohs)
Himeji (HEE-meh-zhee)
shogun (SHOH-guhn) : A military governor who ruled in feudal Japan.

LEARN
Activity 1: Review *(Online)*

Activity 2: How Feudalism Began in Japan *(Online)*

Activity 3: Japanese Castles *(Online)*

Activity 4: Show You Know *(Online)*

Activity 5: History Record Book *(Online)*

Activity 6. Optional: Castle: Japanese Style *(Online)*

Activity 7. Optional: Visiting Scholar *(Online)*

ASSESS
Lesson Assessment: Feudal Japan (*Online*)

You will complete an offline assessment covering the main objectives of this lesson. Your learning coach will score this assessment.

LEARN
Activity 8. Optional: *A Samurai Castle* *(Online)*

Name _____   **Date** _____

A Japanese Castle

Cut out each word below the castle and glue it to the picture where it belongs. Color the castle.

✂ cut

moat ┊ gate ┊ wall

Name _____ Date _____

A Japanese Castle

Read each question and circle the correct answer:

Who lived in these castles?

    peasants   daimyos   emperors

Who gave out the land the castles were built on?

    daimyo   shogun   emperor

What was the one enemy ALL Japanese castles had?

    volcanoes   floods   earthquakes

Lesson Assessment

Feudal Japan

1. What was the man called who commanded the emperor's army and really ruled Japan?

2. What was a daimyo?

3. Which of these buildings is a Japanese castle?

Student Guide
Lesson 5: Life of a Samurai

Lesson Objectives

- Demonstrate mastery of important knowledge and skills taught in previous lessons.
- Define *samurai* as a Japanese warrior.
- Explain that samurai were required to be loyal to their daimyo.
- Define *bushido* as the samurai code of honor.

PREPARE

Approximate lesson time is 60 minutes.

Materials

For the Student
Optional

   🖳 Samurai activity sheet
   🖳 Samurai and Knights activity sheet
   pencils, no. 2
   paper, 8 1/2" x 11"
   pencils, colored, 16 or more
   Elmer's Glue-All
   scissors, round-end safety
   Life Among the Samurai by Eleanor J. Hall

Keywords and Pronunciation

bushido (BOU-shee-doh)
Dajiro (dah-jee-ROH)
Misato (mee-SAH-toh)
samurai (SA-muh-riy) : A Japanese warrior who was required to be loyal to a daimyo.
Taro (TAH-roh)
Tatsujiro (taht-SOO-jee-roh)
Tatsumoto (taht-soo-MOH-toh)

LEARN
Activity 1: Review of Feudal Japan *(Online)*

Activity 2: The Samurai *(Online)*

Activity 3: Show You Know *(Online)*

Activity 4: History Record Book *(Online)*

Activity 5. Optional: Samurai: Japanese Warrior *(Online)*

Activity 6. Optional: Samurai and Knights *(Online)*

ASSESS
Lesson Assessment: Life of a Samurai (*Online*)
You will complete an offline assessment covering the main objectives of this lesson. Your learning coach will score this assessment.

LEARN
Activity 7. Optional: More About Samurai *(Online)*

Name _____   Date _____

Samurai and Knights

Samurai and Knights were alike in many ways. They were also different in some ways. Write the words from the word bank in the column under the picture they go with. Some words belong in both columns.

Samurai

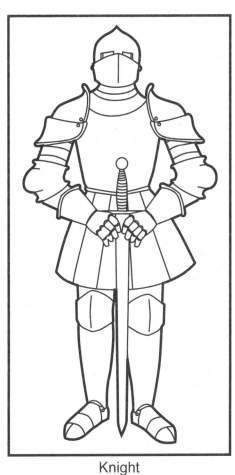

Knight

_____

Word Bank

Europe	bushido	daimyo	sword	Japan	horse	noble	chivalry	armor

Answers: Samurai õ bushido, daimyo, sword, Japan, horse, armor;   Knight õ Europe, sword, horse, noble, chivalry, armor

Samurai: Japanese Warrior

Lesson Assessment

Life of a Samurai

1. What is a samurai?

2. Who were the samurai loyal to?

3. What was bushido?

Student Guide
Lesson 6: Kublai Khan Attacks Twice!

Lesson Objectives

- Demonstrate mastery of important knowledge and skills taught in previous lessons.
- State that Kublai Khan attacked Japan.
- Define *typhoon* as a violent storm having lots of rain and high winds.
- Explain that Kublai Khan's ships were destroyed by typhoons.
- Demonstrate mastery of important knowledge and skills in this semester.
- Demonstrate mastery of important knowledge and skills in this unit.

PREPARE

Approximate lesson time is 60 minutes.

Materials

For the Student

    🖳 From Scandinavia to Japan activity sheet

    map, world

    household items - game die

    scissors, adult

    tape, clear

Keywords and Pronunciation

kamikaze (kah-mih-KAH-zee)

kaze (kah-ZIH)

typhoons (tiy-FOONZ)

LEARN
Activity 1: Review of Kublai Khan *(Online)*

Activity 2: Kublai Khan Reaches Japan *(Online)*

Activity 3: Semester Review: History Record Book *(Online)*

Activity 4. Optional: From Scandinavia to Japan Review Game *(Online)*

✂ cut

B

In the Crusades, who fought against each other?

A. the English and the French
B. European Christians and Muslims
C. shoguns

C

Shinto is Japan's oldest surviving what?

A. empire
B. invention
C. religion

B

Who led armies against each other during the crusades?

A. King John and Ibn Battuta
B. King Richard the Lion-Heart and Saladin
C. Mulan and Kublai Khan

B

In what system did people exchange land, loyalty, and service for protection?

A. Shintoism
B. feudalism
C. civil service

B

What religion started in India and became important in China?

A. Buddhism
B. Shinto
C. Islam

A

What served as both a fortress and a home?

A. cathedrals
B. castles
C. temples

C

Who were Viking explorers?

A. Marco Polo and Ibn Battuta
B. Ibn Sina and Kublai Khan
C. Leif Eriksson and Eric the Red

A

What were Ghana and Mali?

A. medieval African empires
B. medieval Japanese empires
C. Chinese emperors

A

Odin and Thor were what?

A. Viking gods
B. Buddhist heroes
C. Japanese warriors

379

✂ cut

A

What did the Normans do during the Middle Ages?

A. settled in northern France
B. settled in northern Africa
C. settled in northern China

B

Who was Ibn Battuta?

A. a Christian doctor who helped the poor
B. a Muslim explorer who traveled in Africa, Europe, and Asia
C. an explorer from Venice who traveled to China

C

Who led the Normans to conquer England?

A. St. George
B. Saladin
C. William

C

What connected Europe and Asia?

A. the Genghis Khan Route
B. the Marco Polo Highway
C. the Silk Road

C

In what year did King John and his nobles sign the Magna Carta?

A. 476
B. 1066
C. 1215

A

What do we call a military man who ruled medieval Japan?

A. a shogun
B. a daimyo
C. an emperor

A

Which African city was known as a center of trade and learning?

A. Timbuktu
B. Paris
C. Jerusalem

A

What did knights do?

A. sang and entertained kings, queens and lords in their castles
B. farmed the lands around castles where kings, queens and lords lived
C. served kings, queens, and lords and fought their enemies for them

C

Why is China's Song dynasty remembered today?

A. for its many bloody wars
B. for its inventions like the compass
C. for its exploration of Japan

B

✂ cut

A

What was Ethiopia known as during the Middle Ages?

A. a Christian outpost in Africa
B. a Muslim outpost in Africa
C. a Christian outpost in Europe

B

Where did Medieval fairs most often take place?

A. inside a noble's castle
B. in cathedral cities
C. in the market-places of small towns

A

Who attacked Japan two times and had ships that were destroyed by typhoons?

A. Kublai Khan
B. Sundiata, the Lion King of Mali
C. Marco Polo

B

Which two countries fought each other during the Hundred Years War?

A. Japan and China
B. England and France
C. Ghana and Mali

C

What is a samurai?

A. an African king
B. a Buddhist monk
C. a Japanese warrior

A

What did the Mongols do?

A. conquered all of China
B. explore the kingdoms of Mali and Ghana
C. invented fireworks and movable type

A

What is a serf?

A. a peasant who served a noble
B. one of Robin Hood's merry men
C. a musician who entertained nobles

B

To get a job in the government in medieval China, what did people have to do?

A. give gold and silver to the emperor
B. take civil service examinations
C. learn how to make silk

C

What did Joan of Arc do?

A. invade Japan two times
B. defeated Richard Lion-Heart at the Battle of Jerusalem
C. led the French against the English in the Hundred Years War

✂ cut

B

What does the flag of Japan show?

A. a yellow crescent and star on a red background
B. a red circle on a white background
C. a blue circle on a yellow background

B

Which African kingdom did Sundiata become king of?

A. Ethiopia
B. Mali
C. Ghana

C

Where did the Viking gods and goddesses live?

A. Normandy
B. Scandinavia
C. Asgard

B

What did many Vikings live near?

A. deserts
B. fjords
C. rainforests

C

What did merchants traveling to Ghana trade?

A. camels for elephants
B. silver for sugar
C. gold for salt

A

The first castles were made of what?

A. wood
B. cement
C. Legos

C

Who traveled from Venice to China and explored parts of Asia?

A. Leif Eriksson
B. King Lalibela
C. Marco Polo

A

Why did the Chinese build the Great Wall?

A. to keep out invaders
B. to keep in farmers
C. to keep out traders

C

Where did Robin Hood live after he became an outlaw?

A. Smallwood Forest
B. Greatwood Woods
C. Sherwood Forest

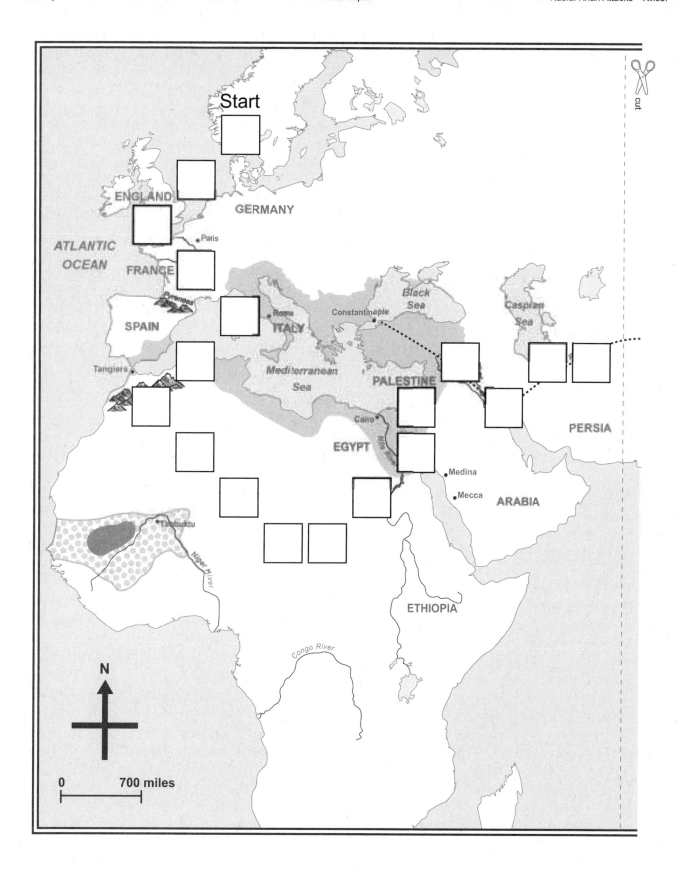

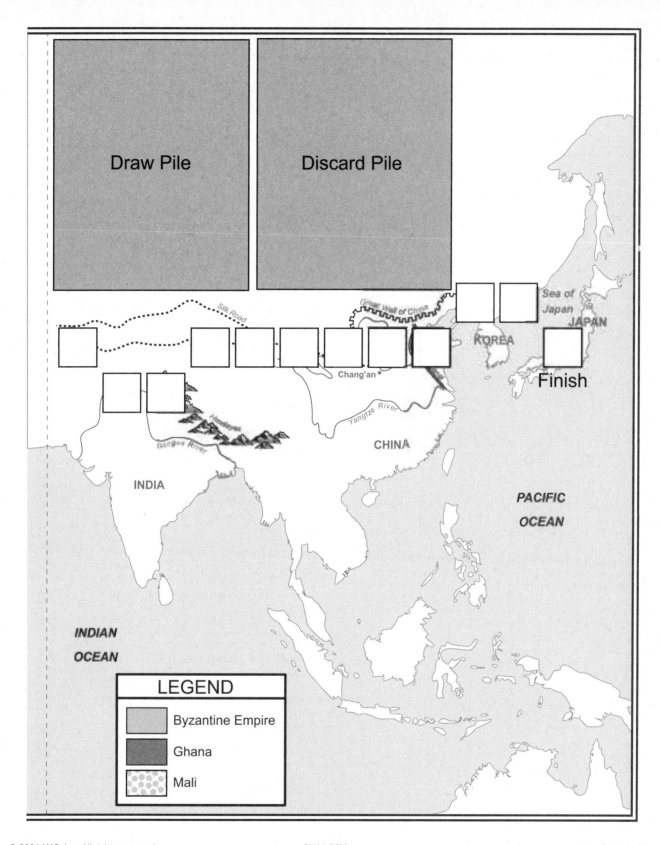

Student Guide
Lesson 7: Semester Assessment

Lesson Objectives

- Demonstrate mastery of important knowledge and skills in this semester.
- Explain that fairs were often held in cathedral cities.
- Identify Erik the Red and Leif Eriksson as Viking explorers.
- State that Kublai Khan attacked Japan.
- Explain that Kublai Khan's ships were destroyed by typhoons.
- Define *samurai* as a Japanese warrior.
- Define a *shogun* as the commander of the army and real ruler of feudal Japan.
- State that Buddhism is a religion that began in India and became important in China.
- Identify the Silk Road as a great overland trade route between Europe and Asia.
- Identify and explain the functions of any two of these inventions that came during the Song dynasty: the compass, paper money, gunpowder, and movable type.
- Identify civil service examinations as tests people took to get jobs in government.
- State that the Mongols conquered all of China.
- Explain that Marco Polo traveled from Venice to China and its large empire.
- State that Marco Polo worked for Kublai Khan in China.
- Explain that Mansa Musa made a famous pilgrimage to Mecca.
- Identify Timbuktu as a center of trade and learning.
- Identify Ibn Battuta as a famous Muslim explorer.
- Explain that Ibn Battuta traveled in Africa, Europe, and Asia.
- Explain that the Crusades were wars between European Christians and Muslims for possession of Palestine and especially for the city of Jerusalem.
- Explain that King Richard I and Saladin led armies against each other during some of the Crusades and then made a truce.
- Identify 1215 as the year the Magna Carta was signed.
- Name England and France as the two countries that fought the Hundred Years' War.
- Explain that Joan of Arc led the French against the English during the end of the Hundred Years' War.
- Identify the Vikings as people who lived near fjords.
- Name at least two of the Viking gods or goddesses.
- Name William the Conqueror as the leader who led the Normans to conquer England.
- Explain that Vikings who settled in northern France were called Normans.
- Identify feudalism as a system in which people exchanged land, loyalty, and service in return for protection.
- Explain that a castle was both a home and a fortress.
- Explain that knights served kings, queens, and lords by fighting their enemies.
- Define *serf* as a peasant who served a noble (lord) by farming the land in exchange for protection.
- Identify Ghana and Mali as medieval African kingdoms.
- Identify Shintoism as Japan's oldest surviving religion.
- Identify Vikings as people who used runes.
- Explain that the flag of Japan shows a rising sun.

PREPARE

Approximate lesson time is 60 minutes.

LEARN
Activity 1: End of Semester! *(Online)*

ASSESS
Semester Assessment: History 2, Semester 2 (*Offline*)

Complete an offline Semester Assessment. Your learning coach will score this part of the assessment.

Name _____   Date _____

Semester 2 Assessment

Read each sentence and its answer choices. Fill in the bubble in front of the word or words that best answer the question.

1. Who were Eric the Red and Leif Eriksson?
   - ○ Viking explorers
   - ○ English kings
   - ○ Chinese monks

2. What was the system in which people exchanged land, loyalty, and service in return for protection?
   - ○ Shintoism
   - ○ feudalism
   - ○ civil service

3. What were the Crusades?
   - ○ wars between English and French nobles for control of France
   - ○ wars between Muslims and European Christians for control of Palestine
   - ○ wars between shoguns for control of the Japanese army and Japan

4. Which of these were medieval African kingdoms?
   - ○ China and Japan
   - ○ Palestine and Jerusalem
   - ○ Ghana and Mali

5. What was the religion that began in India and became important in China?
   - ○ Buddhism
   - ○ Shintoism
   - ○ Islam

6. What is Japan's oldest surviving religion?
   - ○ Shintoism
   - ○ feudalism
   - ○ civil service

7. Which of these were Viking gods?
   - ○ Odin and Thor
   - ○ Buddha and Confucius
   - ○ Lalibela and Mansa Musa

8. What did a castle serve as?
   - ○ a tomb and a resting place
   - ○ a fortress and a home
   - ○ a home and a port

9. Which two people led armies against each other during the Crusades?
   - ○ King John and Ibn Battuta
   - ○ King Richard the Lion-Heart and Saladin
   - ○ Mulan and Kublai Khan

10. What was Timbuktu known as?
   - ○ a center of trade and learning
   - ○ a place to hunt wild game
   - ○ a fortress used to protect Africa

11. What two continents did the Silk Road connect?
   ○ Africa and Europe
   ○ Asia and Australia
   ○ Europe and Asia

12. What do we call the Vikings who settled in northern France during the Middle Ages?
   ○ Normans
   ○ Franks
   ○ Serfs

13. Who served kings, queens, and lords by fighting their enemies for them?
   ○ serfs
   ○ troubadours
   ○ knights

14. What year was the Magna Carta signed?
   ○ 476
   ○ 1066
   ○ 1215

15. Which Muslim explorer traveled in Africa, Europe, and Asia?
   ○ Ibn Battuta
   ○ Ibn Sina
   ○ Marco Polo

16. Why do we remember China's Song dynasty?
- ○ for its many bloody wars
- ○ for inventions like the compass
- ○ for exploration to the tip of Africa

17. What was a shogun?
- ○ a military man and the ruler of Japan
- ○ a peaceful man and a Buddhist monk
- ○ a thoughtful woman and a Japanese scholar

18. Who led the Normans to conquer England?
- ○ Sigurd
- ○ William
- ○ Eleanor

19. What is a serf?
- ○ a craftsman who lived in a town
- ○ a musician who entertained in a castle
- ○ a peasant who served a noble

20. Which two countries fought the Hundred Years War?
- ○ England and France
- ○ England and China
- ○ Japan and China

21. Who took a journey to Mecca, and gave out gold nuggets?
- ○ Sundiata
- ○ Mulan
- ○ Mansa Musa

22. Why did people take civil service examinations in medieval China?
    ○ to get into special schools
    ○ to get jobs in the government
    ○ to get permission to trade goods

23. What is a samurai?
    ○ an African king
    ○ a Chinese soldier
    ○ a Japanese warrior

24. Where did medieval fairs most often take place?
    ○ inside a castle's walls
    ○ in cathedral cities
    ○ in small towns

25. Who led the French against the English during the end of
    the Hundred Years War?
    ○ Genghis Khan
    ○ Richard the Lion-Heart
    ○ Joan of Arc

26. Who conquered all of China?
    ○ the Mongols
    ○ the Crusaders
    ○ the Vikings

27. Who attacked Japan twice but failed to conquer it because his ships were destroyed by typhoons?
    - ○ Kublai Khan
    - ○ Mansa Musa
    - ○ Genghis Khan

28. Who traveled from Venice to China and worked for Kublai Khan?
    - ○ Ibn Battuta
    - ○ Robin Hood
    - ○ Marco Polo

29. Who lived near fjords and used runes?
    - ○ the Mongols
    - ○ the Vikings
    - ○ the Normans

30. Which country has a flag showing a rising sun?
    - ○ China
    - ○ Japan
    - ○ India

Answer Keys

Lesson Assessment Answer Key

Threat from the North: Viking Warriors on the Move

Answers:

1. Vikings

2. North

3. a dragon's head

4. They burned buildings, stole things, and captured and enslaved people.

Lesson Assessment Answer Key

Viking Shipbuilders and Explorers

Answers:

1.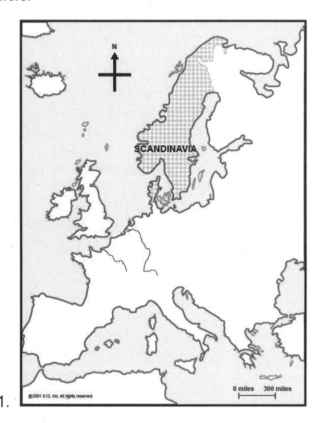

2. The ship in the lower left of the image is a Viking ship.

3. famous Viking explorers

Lesson Assessment Answer Key

Viking Life

Answers:

1. They traded them for other things.

2. near fjords

3. runes

4. Viking runes

Lesson Assessment Answer Key

Viking Gods and Goddesses

Answers:

1. many gods and goddesses

2. at least two of the following: Odin, Thor, Freya, Tyr, and Loki

3. at least two of the following: Tuesday - Tyr; Wednesday - Odin (Woden); Thursday - Thor; Friday - Freya

4. Asgard

Lesson Assessment Answer Key

Buried in Style

Answers:

1. Valhalla

2. Valhalla

3. things the dead would need in the afterlife: clothing, jewelry, animals, wagons

Lesson Assessment Answer Key

The Normans Invade England

Answers:

1. Normandy is in northern France between Britain and the Kingdom of the Franks.

2. Normans

3. William; William the Conqueror; William, Duke of Normandy

Name _____   Date _____

The Viking Challenge

Read each sentence and its answer choices. Fill in the bubble in front the word or words that best answer the question.

1. Which of the following are all Viking gods?
   - ● Loki, Thor, Odin
   - ○ Eric, Tyr, Athena
   - ○ Zeus, Leif, Freya

2. How would you describe Vikings?
   - ○ gentle farmers and herders
   - ● fierce raiders and warriors
   - ○ wise teachers and doctors

3. From which direction did the Vikings come?
   - ● north
   - ○ south
   - ○ west

4. Who were Eric the Red and Leif Eriksson?
   - ○ Norman warriors
   - ● Viking explorers
   - ○ Saxon kings

5. Where did Viking warriors hope to go when they died?
   - ○ to a watery grave
   - ● to Odin's palace named Valhalla
   - ○ to an island in the North Sea

6. Who was the Norman who led his soldiers in battle against England and became its king?
   - ○ Sigurd the Dragon Slayer
   - ○ Thor the Hammer
   - ● William the Conqueror

7. What was the name of the land of the Viking gods and goddesses?
   - ● Asgard
   - ○ Greenland
   - ○ Scandinavia

8. What did Viking raiders travel in?
   - ○ short, slow ships with carved bird heads
   - ○ short, swift ships with carved horse heads
   - ● long, swift ships with carved dragon heads

9. What does this picture show?

   - ○ Greek symbols
   - ○ Egyptian hieroglyphs
   - ● Viking runes

10. Point to Scandinavia on the map.

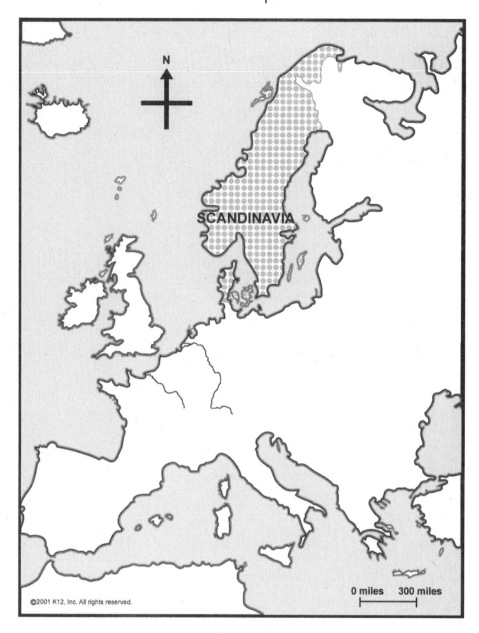

Lesson Assessment Answer Key

What Was Feudalism?

Answers:

1. feudalism

2. king, noble, knight, serf

3. peasants who farmed the land

4. Answers will vary. Acceptable responses could include: Feudalism was a way of life where kings, nobles, knights, and peasants depended on each other. They exchanged land, loyalty, and service in return for protection.

Lesson Assessment Answer Key

Building a Castle

Answers:

1. wood

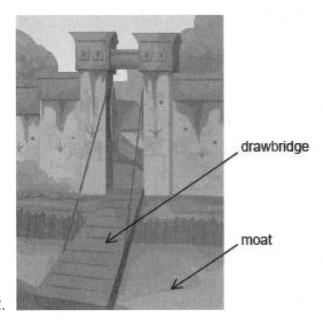

2.

3. to make it harder to attack the castles

4. because stone castles were very hard to attack and enemies could not conquer them in a day or two

Lesson Assessment Answer Key

Life in a Castle

Answers:

1. It was a home as well.

2. nobles or lords, knights, guards, cooks, jesters, servants, and so on

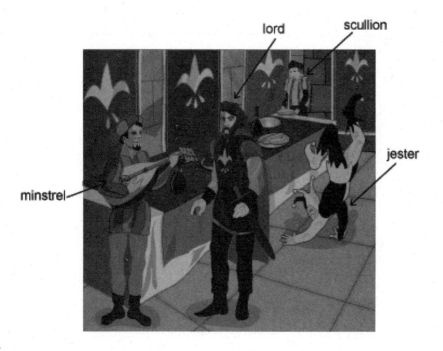

3.

4. the great hall

Lesson Assessment Answer Key

What Is Knighthood?

Answers:

1. kings, queens, or lords, whom knights served by fighting their ruler's enemies in battle

2. The sword and lance are used to battle enemies.

3. to protect themselves

4. the Code of Chivalry

Lesson Assessment Answer Key

A Famous Knight: St. George and the Dragon

Answers:

1. at least two of the following: always fight bravely, keep their promises, help those who need it

2. a person who does great deeds for others

3. He fought and killed the dragon.

Lesson Assessment Answer Key

Supposing You Were a Serf

Answers:

1. a peasant who worked the land for a noble

2. They had to stay and work on the land.

3. Serfs had hard lives. They worked all day and had little freedom.

Lesson Assessment Answer Key

Building a Cathedral

Answers:

1. a large, important church

2. many years

3.

spires

stone sculpture

stained glass windows

Lesson Assessment Answer Key

Come to the Fair!

Answers:

1. to sell goods

2. all over Europe

3. food and entertainment of all kinds--dancers, musicians, games, jousting knights

4. in cities that had cathedrals

Name _____   Date _____

The Feudal World: Answer Key

Read each sentence and its answer choices. Fill in the bubble in front of the word or words that best answer the question.

1. Which of these shows the people listed in order from the most important to the least important, according to the order of rule in feudalism?
   - ○ king, knight, noble, serf
   - ○ serf, noble, king, knight
   - ● king, noble, knight, serf

2. Feudalism meant that people exchanged land, loyalty, and service in return for what?
   - ● protection
   - ○ education
   - ○ money

3. Which of the following is the name for a large, important church with a spire, stained glass windows, and stone sculptures?
   - ○ mosque
   - ● cathedral
   - ○ monastery

4. Who followed a Code of Chivalry and used armor, lances, and swords?
   - ○ serfs
   - ● knights
   - ○ nobles

5. Who farmed the land, were not free, and had a difficult life?

  ● serfs
  ○ knights
  ○ nobles

6. What took place at fairs in the Middle Ages?

  ○ Bishops from western Europe built cathedrals.
  ○ Sailors from the Mediterranean raced ships.
  ● Merchants from all over Europe sold goods.

7. What happened in the legend of Saint George?

  ○ A hardworking serf defeated a dragon.
  ○ A mean noble became a champion.
  ● A brave knight defeated a dragon.

8. What did a castle serve as?

  ○ a tomb and a resting place
  ● a fortress and a home
  ○ a home and a port

9. Why did armies lay siege to stone castles and use weapons such as catapults?

  ● Castles were hard to attack.
  ○ The armies needed to practice.
  ○ It was easy to get into the castles.

10. Eleanor of Aquitaine was queen of which two countries?

  ○ Spain and France
  ○ Italy and England
  ● England and France

Lesson Assessment Answer Key

Command from the Pope

Answers:

1. Jerusalem

2. the Holy Land

3. The Crusades were wars that Christians and Muslims fought for control of Palestine and the city of Jerusalem.

4. control (or possession) of Palestine and Jerusalem

5. a cross

Lesson Assessment Answer Key

Richard the Lion-Heart and Saladin

Answers:

1. Saladin

2. King Richard I

3. They led armies against each other during some of the crusades and made a truce.

Lesson Assessment Answer Key

The Legend of Robin Hood

Answers:

1. Robin Hood

2. in Sherwood Forest

3. They met when they fought on a footbridge.

Lesson Assessment Answer Key

King John and the Magna Carta

Answers:

1. England

2. Answers may vary but must include: The Magna Carta was a guarantee of rights that even the king had to obey.

   Sample answer:
   The Magna Carta said that even a king had to obey the law, that nobles had rights too, that kings couldn't take money from nobles without permission, and that kings couldn't punish people without a fair trial.

3. 1215

Lesson Assessment Answer Key

The Hundred Years' War

Answers:

1. England and France

2. Acceptable answers include: for control of France (or Aquitane).

3. the longbow and the cannon

Lesson Assessment Answer Key

Joan of Arc: The Girl Who Saved France

Answers:

1. the French

2. visions; visions of the Archangel Michael

3. France

Lesson Assessment Answer Key

Towns and Trade

Answers:

1. People came together because they had things to sell to each other. People arrived to sell their products.

2. They had lots of shops; they were crowded; they were surrounded by walls; they were dirty; they had twisting, narrow streets.

3. trade and craftsmanship

Name _____   Date _____

Crusades Abroad and Changes in Europe: Answer Key

Read each sentence and its answer choices. Fill in the bubble in front of the word or words that best answer the question.

1. What were the Crusades?
   - ○ wars between the English and the French for possession of France
   - ● wars between Muslims and European Christians for possession of Palestine
   - ○ wars between King John and his nobles for possession of England

2. Which two countries fought each other in the Hundred Years' War?
   - ○ England and Spain
   - ○ Italy and France
   - ● England and France

3. In what year was the Magna Carta signed?
   - ● 1215
   - ○ 1492
   - ○ 1776

4. Which of the following choices correctly describes medieval towns?
   - ○ They were surrounded by walls and were very clean.
   - ● They were very dirty and had twisting, narrow streets.
   - ○ They had wide, straight streets and had lots of shops.

5. What city is sacred to Jews, Muslims, and Christians?
   - ○ Constantinople
   - ○ Paris
   - ● Jerusalem

6. What was the name of the plague that killed many people during the Middle Ages?

   ○ the Rat Plague

   ● the Black Death

   ○ the Dark Boils Sickness

7. Who had visions and led the French against the English during the Hundred Years' War?

   ○ Saladin

   ○ Prince Charles

   ● Joan of Arc

8. What English king became known as the "Lion-Heart" and fought in the Crusades?

   ● Richard

   ○ John

   ○ Charlemagne

9. Who lived in Sherwood Forest and stole from the rich to give to the poor?

   ○ Joan of Arc

   ● Robin Hood

   ○ King John

10. Who was forced to sign the Magna Carta?

   ● King John

   ○ King Richard

   ○ Prince Charles

Lesson Assessment Answer Key

Welcome to Africa!

Answers:

1. The Sahara is the large area of desert in northern Africa.

2. Acceptable answers include dry, sandy, hot, rocky, no water.

3. flat, with lots of grass

4. The Nile River is in northeastern Africa.
   The Niger River is in western Africa.
   The Congo River is in the middle of Africa.

Lesson Assessment Answer Key

Ghana: A Gold Kingdom

Answers:

1. in western Africa

2. gold

3. salt

4. camels

Name _____   Date _____

Lesson Assessment Answer Key

Sundiata: Lion King of Mali

Answers:

1. Mali

2. Africa

3. Sundiata could not walk or talk.

Lesson Assessment Answer Key

Mansa Musa of Mali

Answers:

1. Mansa Musa

2. He was very rich.

3. to Mecca

Lesson Assessment Answer Key

All the Way to Timbuktu

Answers:

1. Timbuktu is on the Niger River in the west African country of Mali. It is just east of Ghana on the map.

2. the Niger River

3. People took them there for trade.

4. Timbuktu was a great center of learning.

Lesson Assessment Answer Key

Ibn Battuta: An Amazing Traveler

Answers:

1. Ibn Battuta was famous for being a traveler and an explorer.

2. Islam

3. Egypt, Mecca, Spain, China, Mali, and others

Name _____   Date _____

Medieval African Empires

Read each sentence and its answer choices. Fill in the bubble in front the word or words that best answer the question.

1. The Kingdoms of Ghana and Mali, and the city of Timbuktu grew up along the _____ River.
   - ○ Nile
   - ● Niger
   - ○ Congo

2. In Ghana merchants traded
   - ○ cotton for jewels
   - ○ salt for furs
   - ● gold for salt

3. Muslim merchants traveled across north Africa using
   - ● camel caravans
   - ○ sailing ships
   - ○ covered wagons

4. Mansa Musa was known throughout Africa and Europe as a wealthy king who
   - ○ led his people to victory during the Crusades
   - ● went on pilgrimage to Mecca and gave away gold
   - ○ started the kingdom of Mali by defeating Sumanguru

5. Sundiata was
- ● known as Mali's founder and also as the "Lion King"
- ○ the explorer who discovered the Nile River
- ○ a person who founded a new religion

6. Ibn Battuta
- ○ wanted to travel but never crossed the Sahara
- ● explored Africa and the world for more than 25 years
- ○ was the largest city in Ghana

7. The Sahara is a
- ● desert
- ○ plain
- ○ hill

8. A city in Africa famous for its trade and learning was:
- ● Timbuktu
- ○ Mali
- ○ Ghana

9. The part of Africa called the savanna is
- ○ swamp
- ○ mountain
- ● grassland

Lesson Assessment Answer Key

Remembering Ancient China

Answers:

1. China is in the lower right hand corner of the map. It is east of India and west of the Pacific Ocean.

2. silk

3. Acceptable answers may include: The Chinese found the worms on the mulberry trees. They learned how to twist the worm threads into silk threads. They made silk cloth from the thread.

4. Confucius

5. the Great Wall of China

Lesson Assessment Answer Key

The Grand Canal

Answers:

1. The Yellow River is just south of the Gobi Desert and the Great Wall of China. It is the northern of the two Chinese rivers on the map. It runs parallel to the Yangtze River to its south.

2. The Yangtze River in in central China. It is the southern of the two Chinese rivers on the map. It runs parallel to the Yellow River to its north.

3. They built the Grand Canal.

4. rice

5. A dynasty is a family that rules for many years.

Lesson Assessment Answer Key

Buddhism in China

Answers:

1. India

2. Buddha

3. Many Chinese people became Buddhists.

Lesson Assessment Answer Key

The Trading Tang: The Silk Road

Answers:

1. The Silk Road runs east/west between Chang'an in China (through northern India, Persia and Arabia) and Constantinople on the Black and Mediterranean Seas.

2. Europe and Asia

3. Merchants used the Silk Road to transport, or carry, silk and many other things to trade.

4. the Tang Dynasty

5. The Tang emperors made the Silk Road safe by sending soldiers to guard it.

Lesson Assessment Answer Key

Mulan

Answers:

1. Mulan

2. It is a story.

3. Mulan disguised herself as a man.

4. Mulan fought bravely, became a general, and helped China beat the invaders.

Name _____ Date _____

Lesson Assessment Answer Key

The Inventive Song Dynasty

Answers:

1. The Song dynasty was famous for inventions.

2. Acceptable answers include gunpowder, the compass, movable type, and paper money.

3. Compass: finding their way on sea and land. Gunpowder: fighting in wars, fireworks. Movable type: made printing easier, so people could have more books. Paper money: made trade easier.

Lesson Assessment Answer Key

Mongols on the March: Genghis Khan

Answers:

1. Genghis Khan

2. Chinese

Lesson Assessment Answer Key

Kublai Khan

Answers:

1. the Mongols

2. Kublai Khan

Lesson Assessment Answer Key

Marco Polo: Man of a Million Stories

Answers:

1. Marco Polo

2. Marco Polo went to China and told fabulous stories when he came back.

3. Marco Polo began his travels in Venice. He traveled to China and through other parts of Asia.

4. Kublai Khan

Name _____   **Date** _____

Medieval China

Read each sentence and its answer choices. Fill in the bubble in front of the word or words that best answer the question.

1. Why is the finely made pottery called porcelain also known as "china"?
   - ○ The Chinese captured the inventor.
   - ○ The Chinese bought the right to name it that.
   - ● The Chinese invented it.

2. Who was a great Chinese teacher?
   - ○ Mansa Musa
   - ○ Marco Polo
   - ● Confucius

3. What was the name of the man-made waterway built to connect the Yellow and Yangtze Rivers?
   - ○ the Panama Canal
   - ● the Grand Canal
   - ○ the Yalu Connector

4. What religion began in India and later became important in China?
   - ○ Christianity
   - ○ Judaism
   - ● Buddhism

5. What is the name of the overland trade route that connected Asia and Europe?
   - ● the Silk Road
   - ○ the Tang Trail
   - ○ the China Highway

6. Who was the first Mongol emperor of China?
   ○ Confucius
   ● Kublai Khan
   ○ Mansa Musa

7. Which of these Chinese inventions helped people, especially sailors, find their way?
   ● compass
   ○ movable type
   ○ gunpowder

8. During which dynasty were paper money, compasses, and fireworks invented?
   ● Song
   ○ Chin
   ○ Han

9. What traveler and explorer left his home in Venice and spent twenty years traveling to China and other parts of Asia?
   ○ Sundiata
   ○ Mulan
   ● Marco Polo

10. Who was the founder of the Mongol Empire?
    ● Genghis Khan
    ○ Immanuel Kant
    ○ Hari Khan

Lesson Assessment Answer Key

Japan: The Island Kingdom

Answers:

1. observation

2. observation

3. a group of islands

4. four

5. Mount Fuji

Lesson Assessment Answer Key

Shinto: An Ancient Japanese Religion

Answers:

1. Shinto

2. Kami

3. the wooden gate, or torii

Name _____ Date _____

Lesson Assessment Answer Key

Buddhism in Japan

Answers:

1. People brought it to Japan from China and other parts of Asia.
2. the Great Buddha at Kamakura
3. a pagoda

Lesson Assessment Answer Key

Feudal Japan

Answers:

1. the shogun

2. a person who owned a lot of land in feudal Japan; like a noble

3. The picture on the left is the Japanese castle.

Lesson Assessment Answer Key

Life of a Samurai

Answers:

1. a Japanese warrior

2. their daimyo

3. the samurai code of honor

Name _____   Date _____

Semester 2 Assessment

Read each sentence and its answer choices. Fill in the bubble in front of the word or words that best answer the question.

1. Who were Eric the Red and Leif Eriksson?
   - ● Viking explorers
   - ○ English kings
   - ○ Chinese monks

2. What was the system in which people exchanged land, loyalty, and service in return for protection?
   - ○ Shintoism
   - ● feudalism
   - ○ civil service

3. What were the Crusades?
   - ○ wars between English and French nobles for control of France
   - ● wars between Muslims and European Christians for control of Palestine
   - ○ wars between shoguns for control of the Japanese army and Japan

4. Which of these were medieval African kingdoms?
   - ○ China and Japan
   - ○ Palestine and Jerusalem
   - ● Ghana and Mali

5. What was the religion that began in India and became important in China?
- ● Buddhism
- ○ Shintoism
- ○ Islam

6. What is Japan's oldest surviving religion?
- ● Shintoism
- ○ feudalism
- ○ civil service

7. Which of these were Viking gods?
- ● Odin and Thor
- ○ Buddha and Confucius
- ○ Lalibela and Mansa Musa

8. What did a castle serve as?
- ○ a tomb and a resting place
- ● a fortress and a home
- ○ a home and a port

9. Which two people led armies against each other during the Crusades?
- ○ King John and Ibn Battuta
- ● King Richard the Lion-Heart and Saladin
- ○ Mulan and Kublai Khan

10. What was Timbuktu known as?
- ● a center of trade and learning
- ○ a place to hunt wild game
- ○ a fortress used to protect Africa

11. What two continents did the Silk Road connect?
   - ○ Africa and Europe
   - ○ Asia and Australia
   - ● Europe and Asia

12. What do we call the Vikings who settled in northern France during the Middle Ages?
   - ● Normans
   - ○ Franks
   - ○ Serfs

13. Who served kings, queens, and lords by fighting their enemies for them?
   - ○ serfs
   - ○ troubadours
   - ● knights

14. What year was the Magna Carta signed?
   - ○ 476
   - ○ 1066
   - ● 1215

15. Which Muslim explorer traveled in Africa, Europe, and Asia?
   - ● Ibn Battuta
   - ○ Ibn Sina
   - ○ Marco Polo

16. Why do we remember China's Song dynasty?
    - ○ for its many bloody wars
    - ● for inventions like the compass
    - ○ for exploration to the tip of Africa

17. What was a shogun?
    - ● a military man and the ruler of Japan
    - ○ a peaceful man and a Buddhist monk
    - ○ a thoughtful woman and a Japanese scholar

18. Who led the Normans to conquer England?
    - ○ Sigurd
    - ● William
    - ○ Eleanor

19. What is a serf?
    - ○ a craftsman who lived in a town
    - ○ a musician who entertained in a castle
    - ● a peasant who served a noble

20. Which two countries fought the Hundred Years War?
    - ● England and France
    - ○ England and China
    - ○ Japan and China

21. Who took a journey to Mecca, and gave out gold nuggets?
    - ○ Sundiata
    - ○ Mulan
    - ● Mansa Musa

22. Why did people take civil service examinations in medieval China?
   - ○ to get into special schools
   - ● to get jobs in the government
   - ○ to get permission to trade goods

23. What is a samurai?
   - ○ an African king
   - ○ a Chinese soldier
   - ● a Japanese warrior

24. Where did medieval fairs most often take place?
   - ○ inside a castle's walls
   - ● in cathedral cities
   - ○ in small towns

25. Who led the French against the English during the end of the Hundred Years War?
   - ○ Genghis Khan
   - ○ Richard the Lion-Heart
   - ● Joan of Arc

26. Who conquered all of China?
   - ● the Mongols
   - ○ the Crusaders
   - ○ the Vikings

27. Who attacked Japan twice but failed to conquer it because his ships were destroyed by typhoons?
- ● Kublai Khan
- ○ Mansa Musa
- ○ Genghis Khan

28. Who traveled from Venice to China and worked for Kublai Khan?
- ○ Ibn Battuta
- ○ Robin Hood
- ● Marco Polo

29. Who lived near fjords and used runes?
- ○ the Mongols
- ● the Vikings
- ○ the Normans

30. Which country has a flag showing a rising sun?
- ○ China
- ● Japan
- ○ India